WITHDRAWN

D0960797

Group Therapy for the Adolescent

Group Therapy for the Adolescent

Edited by
Norman S. Brandes, M.D.
and
Malcolm L. Gardner, Ph.D.

Jason Aronson, Inc.
New York

Library of Congress Catalog Card Number :
72- 94845
ISBN : 0-87668-060-0

Designed by Jennifer Mellen

Manufactured in the United States of America

Contributors

Ernest E. Andrews, M.S.W.

Program Director
The Family Institute
Cincinnati, Ohio

Henry R. Angelino, Ph.D.

Professor of Psychology
Ohio State University
Columbus, Ohio

Fern J. Azima, Ph.D.

Assistant Professor
Department of Psychiatry
McGill University
Montreal, Canada

Norman S. Brandes, M.D.

Associate Clinical Professor
Department of Psychiatry
Ohio State University
and private practice of
psychiatry
Columbus, Ohio

Malcolm L. Gardner, Ph.D.

Associate Professor
Department of Psychiatry
Ohio State University
Columbus, Ohio

Kathleen Gideon, A.T.R.

Department of Psychology
Columbia University
New York, New York

Irvin A. Kraft, M.D.   Associate Professor of Psychiatry
and Pediatrics
Baylor College of Medicine
Houston, Texas

Beryce W. MacLennan, Ph.D. Mental Health Study Center
NIMH
Adelphi, Maryland

Joann Vick, A.C.S.W.   Instructor in Social Work
Baylor College of Medicine
Houston, Texas

Table of Contents

Preface

Over the past decade group therapy has experienced a
rapid growth, and has considerably broadened its theoretical
base. In this book the editors have presented a wide spectrum of the approaches currently used in the group treatment of emotionally disturbed adolescents.

An accurate understanding of the environment faced
by all adolescents in today's world, from which the disturbed
adolescent deviates or develops his pathology, is a prerequisite for the therapist working with disturbed youth. It
is for this reason we chose to open the book with a chapter
by an author experienced and knowledgeable in adolescent
dynamics, but in no way identified directly with its deviant
or pathological segments.

15

Dr. Angelino's chapter provides a "normal" emotional-cultural baseline of today's adolescent from which the emotionally disturbed adolescent departs. He points out that, since World War II, the essence of American society and culture has been the phenomenon of rapid and extensive changes, brought about by an advanced industrial, urban-technological society. Youth culture, a reaction to this phenomenon and the resulting delay in the completion of adolescence, has become world wide. Within the boundaries of this new and complex culture are subcultures, which include young people who cannot cope with the conflicts within themselves and with their peer groups. The drug subculture has not been included, to any great extent, in the following chapters, for two reasons:

(1) When a young patient is under the influence of drugs such as speed or LSD, psychotherapy will not be meaningful to him because psychotherapy cannot compete with these drugs any more than it can compete with the effects of a series of mind-scrambling electric shocks.

(2) Once the young patient agrees to stay off drugs and keeps this contract with the therapist, then the various treatment ideas described in this book will apply to him, as to any other young patient.

The remaining chapters of this book are devoted to the variety of group therapy approaches that are available to mental health professionals to help them help their young disturbed patients develop a reasonable sense of belonging with their peer group, or carry them through the rest of adolescence to the more settled, less volatile years of adulthood.

Because teenagers express themselves in relation to the community and are treated as problems by the community, it seems important in this day and age to discuss the group treatment of adolescents who are community problems. Dr.

MacLennan, deeply involved in working with community youth groups for many years, and the author of publications on group treatment of socially deprived and "delinquent" youth groups, presents a condensed, yet broad version of the many things going on in these group activities.

From socially deprived and community groups, the reader is invited to absorb the third chapter on College Students by Dr. Malcolm L. Gardner. A campus psychologist and on the campus scene (right in the middle, usually) for more years than he cares to admit, Dr. Gardner agrees with the co-editor of this book that many professionals "doing adolescent groups" are really working with the 18 to 21 year old college age bracket. College students often set the rules and provide the nearest and (most of the time) the best identification models for their younger high and junior high school counterparts. Too often, psychiatric residents, psychologists, and social workers rush at the opportunity to work with college student groups because they are "fun" groups—after all, they are so smart, attractive, educated, and witty! Dr. Gardner points out the other side of the coin, with a reminder that all is not "fun" in working through the complex of emotional difficulties of college students.

To our best knowledge, S. R. Slavson, one of the pioneers in group therapy in this country, was the first to use the term para-analytic in reference to adolescent group therapy. Dr. Brandes, long an admirer of Mr. Slavson, has practiced and taught his group therapy ideas over the years, and gradually developed modifications. For example, chapter four describes multidimensional therapy, a variety of combinations of family, individual, and group therapy for one or both parents, which goes on simultaneously with the treatment of the adolescent. Experiences and ideas on balance, selection, procedure, and rules, as well as defining goals, are taken up in this chapter in as common sensical a manner as possible.

The two chapters on the use of creative expression in working with teenagers, show the importance of these vast therapy territories that need more interested and trained mental health people for further development and refinement. The possibilities are great because most adolescent patients really "dig" these therapy approaches and they serve as ideal bridges to the more difficult dynamic, verbal, group communication of feelings, insight, and interaction. An adequate background of training in psychotherapy methods becomes the major prerequisite if creative, expressive, groups are to become serious therapy groups. The alternative is that damage to patients can occur if therapists misinterpret expressiveness, or interpret without really understanding the history and makeup of the patient. Here is another responsibility of the therapist—to see to it that he is prepared (or properly supervised) before he tackles a particular kind of therapy.

The concept of responsibility in therapy is implied or defined throughout this book, but especially in the chapters on the para-analytical approach, and transference and countertransference. The last chapter is devoted, for the most part, to the responsibility of the therapist to himself and his young patients. Too often we take for granted that young patients can't see us as well as older ones can and we think that young patients feel that our defects and problems as human beings don't really count.

This book says they count. Dr. Azima goes quite thoroughly into the problems of the therapist who is performing his healing arts in the hall of mirrors of young patients' groups. Sooner or later, the therapist who projects his home movies on the screens of his young patients, finds himself in difficulty.

Our objective has been a readable book both in its overall length and in the method of presentation. The individual contributors were asked to confine their chapters, as much as possible, to observations from their own experiences—avoiding, where possible, the use of technical terminology, historical and theoretical discussion, research presentation and evaluation, and literature reviews. The clinical material presented has been carefully disguised without distorting its accuracy, and in no way can it be identified with actual persons.

N.S.B.

M.L.G.

Contemporary Adolescence

HENRY R. ANGELINO, PH.D.

Adolescence, which is only one phase of the developmental life cycle, has managed, in recent years, to become a phenomenon of great concern to all adults. In America, it is primarily an artifact of our modern industrial, urban, and technological society, and it is a significant product of the great affluence in this country following World War II.

INDUSTRIALIZATION AND AFFLUENCE

Ever since the forties, American science has produced some of the most significant and creative developments in

21

world technology, from which, eventually, will evolve a whole new society. Signs are appearing here and there pointing to changes that will become our future life style. Furthermore, these past decades have included a period of great turmoil with the post World War II period of rapid technological and social changes, challenging both adults and youth. The consistent demands of equality of opportunity and equal status by our large minority groups further emphasize and continue the turmoil of the past decades.

America, currently the world's leading industrial-technological society, has championed industrialism as the key to its system while making capitalism the philosophical means of fulfilling its industrial destiny. Ours is also a society of great mobility, beginning with the great depression of the thirties, into the war years, and then through the decades following the war. People, especially the college age youth and the upward bound young adults, are changing their places of residence quite rapidly due to increasing economic and other opportunities that reach beyond the confines of their communities and even their native states. Mass education has made for greater mobility when local areas can no longer provide adequate employment.

Post war affluence has also created a new social class, that of the highly skilled technician with his increased income, permitting better living conditions, better opportunities for his children, more leisure time and more need satisfactions. In general, America is becoming a nation of all native-born persons who owe their allegiance to it regardless of ethnic or racial backgrounds. The youth of today who make up these variations in backgrounds are far less concerned about these differences as they are with the entire "stream" of American culture, which they insist on challenging as quite irrelevant and unappealing.

This introductory chapter is concerned with what might be termed our "typical" adolescent, who, despite the current social scene, has managed to come through his so-called "crisis period" without too many permanent scars. We want to look at this majority who eventually will "make it" despite the frustrations, disillusionments, and upheavals of the past decade. The large number of these youth feel that contemporary American culture (the system) is far too materialistic, bent on selfish motives, and lacking sensitivity and commitment to the requirements of the younger generation. Youth, in general, has shown a willingness to learn about the whole of our society, to accept responsibility, and, generally, to try to fit into the system—to belong. They also expect a greater degree of independence than given to their adolescent ancestors, and a real concern for them as individuals, as human beings, not as marginal people whom present day adults consider as those who have not yet left childhood nor yet entered complete adulthood. They do not want to be ignored, pushed aside, or treated as outsiders to the system.

LET ADOLESCENTS BECOME ADEQUATE ADULTS

A well known truism worth repeating is that in every known society the parental aim is to raise their children to become adults capable of assuming the prescribed adult roles and capable of becoming part of the particular social system. The "adequate adult," then, is the goal of all societies. The parents are charged with fulfilling this requirement; with carrying out, as best they can, this process of socialization. The family, however defined, is, in all societies, the basic social unit responsible for the individual's early training. In America, the basic unit is the nuclear family, composed of two generations only—the parents and off-spring, a highly mobile and self-contained unit primarily dependent upon itself for life's satisfactions. In this setting, the new-born gradually learns his way around the world. American culture is mainly that of the "Middle Class" who for so long has acted under the assumption that its attitudes, its values, its morality, is the public morality. With the new affluence of the past quarter-century, new classes have emerged and moved into prominence with their variety of groupings. In the foreground is the new class of our youth, a significantly large segment of our population, better educated, better trained, and better moneyed than any previous generation. All these changes have become particularly evident in contemporary American society.

YOUTH CULTURE IS WORLD WIDE

This new class—youth culture—is really not a class phenomenon but a generational phenomenon and actually is visible all over the world. It is distinctly a modern phenomenon and is present in every country that has taken the industrial-technological route. In Europe, this youth culture may be seen in Britain, France, Italy, West Germany, in Russia and its satellites. In Asia, it is seen in Japan, China, India, and in many of the Southeast Asian countries. Youth culture is truly an institution characteristic of advanced industrialization.

"TIMES HAVE CHANGED"

Any attempt to understand this rise of youth culture must, of course, take into consideration the tremendous transformations that have occurred during this twentieth century that is not yet three-fourths completed. These changes include our rapidly advancing technological accomplishments, most of which have eliminated unskilled and semi-skilled jobs; our mass production techniques that are producing degrees of alienation from the actual means of production, and that are producing alienation from work itself. The variety of highly paid routine work, so necessary in assembly-line production, ends up being boring, unchallenging, and without genuine satisfaction to the worker. Recently, there have been warnings that assembly lines will be eliminated in order to rectify the dehumanizing effect on the workers.

ENFORCED EXTENSION OF ADOLESCENCE

Technology and advanced industrialization have created a vacuum in the work world for most youth. This technological revolution has eliminated many jobs that a short generation ago were quite numerous. No longer can youth find jobs readily; no longer can they learn future occupational roles by participation, and, most significant, no longer are they really needed in the economy that increasingly depends upon automation for its life. Thus, over the years, there has been an enforced extension of adolescence in western society to at least a decade longer than in former times. The adolescent enculturation process has been extended in age to the middle twenties—longer in many professional cases—after which the individual can be considered to be ready for his adult role. First it was acceptable to complete education through high school; now it's through college—the college degree is currently the desired norm, but what then? A college degree is no longer an auto-

CONTEMPORARY ADOLESCENCE   25

matic guarantee of a job, as witness the numbers of college graduates without gainful employment, regardless of their educational backgrounds.

YOUTH CULTURE FILLS A GAP IN LIFE

As technology becomes more complex, requirements will necessarily increase, requiring more years to adequately prepare for adult occupational participation. Adolescence had to be extended to delay the time when the individual could become economically independent. With this enforced adolescence, we witness the development of youth groups, forming what is known as youth culture (sub-culture would be more precise), with its own set of values, norms and life styles, and with behaviors that differ somewhat from those of the adult culture, but patterned after the adult norms. This set of behaviors, covert and overt, serves to identify a distinct socio-psychological phase of life. We are seeing our young people, both male and female, trying desperately to achieve some form of self-identity, some feeling of belong-ingness, within this uncertain and ambiguous period of wars, hunger, poverty amidst affluence, and minority demands of equal rights and opportunities.

Sociologists have told us how youth groups develop. Whenever and wherever the family or the kinship unit cannot or does not provide the attainment of full social status for its membership, other units gradually arise to provide this function. In complex industrial societies like ours, membership in the larger group does not require belonging to any such groupings beyond a certain age, for example, childhood. In addition, we delegate to specialized groups, institutions, such as school, church, political parties, government, the authority to perform the major educational, religious, and political functions necessary to adult life. In

Russia the nursery schools for two-year-olds and up are institutionalized to perform these functions. In parts of Israel the various kibbutzim carry out the task of enculturating the young through adolescence.

LIFE BETWEEN TWO WORLDS

In all industrialized countries the peer group, or one's age-mates, provides the transition phase between the two worlds of an individual—the world of the child and the world of the adult. The adolescent, of course, is in neither world and finds himself in this position because of certain cultural conditions inherent in all advanced industrial-technological societies. Peers then take on specific importance to the adolescent. With them the individual can find, eventually, his or her own identity with persons more like oneself. Peers may, and often do, take priority over home, school, and church in their demands for the complete allegiance of their membership. On the positive side, peer groups aid in furthering the individual's emancipation from his family; they provide opportunities for maturing relationships with age-mates, including experiences with the opposite sex, eventually providing opportunities for more experience in mate selection. They also give strong support to those questioning and challenging adult values and behaviors. Peers become, in reality, the "significant others" for personal relationships outside the nuclear family. These various groupings provide, in many different ways, opportunities for adolescents to achieve some form of self-identity and meaning, while going through the phase of experimentation with somewhat different values and attitudes than those of the major culture around them. Note the wide range of youth groups existing throughout the world—each with its own particular patternings and behavioral objectives—and a true appreciation of the extent of peer group-ings will be obtained.

In general, peer groups may be likened to a double-edged sword. They work in both a positive and a negative fashion, though the former is more the norm. They serve as a necessary support during the long and sometimes difficult move toward adulthood. They provide the necessary media for the adolescent's need for self-expression, which some-times leads to socially deviant expressions. In addition, peer groups provide opportunities for differences in attitudes, as well as modes of dress, speech, music, various fads, and specialized dating patterns, all of which are somewhat com-mon to all youth in every industrialized nation.

WHAT'S A TYPICAL ADOLESCENT?

Turning from the socio-cultural scene to the young human being we want to examine; a concept so often ex-pressed by adults and adolescents alike is raised. What is the typical or average adolescent like? What is typical, what is average? As adults, we must remember that what was called "typical" in our adolescent days no longer holds true today, in describing the present generation of adolescents. Today's parents (of adolescents) were themselves adolescents in the late thirties and in the forties. The outside world, then, was considerably different from today, in technology, in values and beliefs, and in various behavior patterns. The elements of mass media were either on the drawing board or in their infancy. The automobile, which radically changed our whole living pattern, was not the main medium of trans-portation. Television, advanced electronics, and the mass produced solid-state portable radios were non-existent. The atomic bomb and atomic power were unknown, the airplane was in its infancy, and automation a thing of the distant future. What contemporary adolescents take for granted today was almost non-existent during the adolescence of their parents. No wonder, then, that we do have a "conflict of generations." From the more or less jaundiced eyes of adults, today's young people are something out of this world.

In reality, most young Americans are not of either extreme, neither right nor left, but within the broader spectrum of the "middle," leaning sometimes a little to the right and sometimes a little to the left, but seldom far enough either way to make much difference. Most seem pretty much aware of the tenor of the times and of the uncertain future. They are not necessarily frightened by the current scene but they are concerned about the present and, more so, about the future. They want some stability in this system of rapid change.

ADOLESCENTS AND "THE SYSTEM"

Young people are genuinely concerned about the quality of the future, but so many of them, seemingly, show no overt conflict with "the system," though conflicts may exist. These conflicts are covert, under-the-surface feelings and resentments that are kept under control and never shown. They are not sold on the system but since it is the only one around, they try very hard to accommodate to it. There are numerous ambivalences and conflicts but these eventually become internalized and kept under some control. However, note the often heard complaint of being "caught up in this rat race," of reports of hating their enforced roles, but they are going ahead and trying to ready themselves for the very uncertain future. Witness also the great sigh of relief upon graduation! A favorite admonition of young people is "keep your cool"—don't go overboard about anything!

Here, we stated some of the behaviors of our typical young people of today. The great majority neither explode nor give up, but rather keep on going, grinding out what they must in the hope that their future will be somewhat different from the present. To be sure, this is not without some occasional protestations; some frustrations, some conflicts about this whole value system of ours, the products of which they often find irrelevant and incomprehensible. Yet, they persist and eventually they, too, will become part of the system, adapting to it and occupying various roles within it. Hopefully, these newcomers to the system will be willing to create positive values and new changes to make a better world for the next generation.

Contemporary Problems

BERYCE W. MACLENNAN, PH.D.

It has become a truism that adolescence is an age of change and transition, and an age of rapid personal development, individuation, and reassessment of values. Because of the urge to separate from the family, many normally developing youth go through a period of rejecting and defying current family and community ways and are consequently seen as social problems. Many youth become interested in some current social movement. Some of these who are more intra-psychically disturbed carry their actions to extremes. Other adolescents, who, for one reason or another, have had long standing difficulty in performing adequately, find deviant ways to obtain social status, success, and material advantage. Some teenagers are seen as problems merely because their life style is contrary to that of the community in which they live. Because all such youth express themselves in relation to the community and are defined as problems by the community (sometimes adults talk as if this included all youth), the particular mode of expression varies from place to place and over time.

COMMON PRESENT DAY PROBLEMS

If we look at delinquency in present day America, we find several different groups of problems; the classic problems of poor boys and girls who devote themselves to careers in crime as the best possible alternative to a life of poverty; some from all walks of life who temporarily express their need for defiance and excitement through breaking the law; others, still, who express their intrapsychic difficulties through crime. However, today there are also some teenagers, often quite affluent, who adopt internecine warfare or more impersonal violence as a means of expressing their anger and despair with modern civilization. The age old problems of the delinquent, the sexual deviant, and the alcoholic pale beside the much more aggressive and violent protests that engage society today.

Youth's rejection of present day society is being expressed by many in aggressive action; in large scale running away from home to youth rallying points in large cities where life is lived in violation of adult accepted mores; in experimentation with drug taking; in violent protest against the social policies of the day, particularly those that affect youth personally, such as the draft, the war in Vietnam, and racial discrimination.

There are many explanations of these phenomena. The

long dependency in which young people are kept today frequently does not permit them to become self-supporting or to have a significant role in society until an age at which, in other eras, they would have expended half their adult lives. The longer life span of adults reduces the speed of advancement for youth. The impersonality and mobility of modern society releases youth from tight, adult, neighborhood control, and also promotes feelings of confusion, loneliness, and alienation. The expectation of material gratification for all members of society, of all economic, racial, ethnic, religious, and sex groups, creates disappointment and frustration when barriers are encountered and the expectation goes unfulfilled.

THERAPEUTIC RESPONSES TO THE PROBLEMS

What, then, have been the responses of the psychotherapeutic world to the personal and community problems presented by these youth? It has been widely recognized in recent years that such youth are not willing to see themselves as problems and patients, and are not appropriately treated in regular psychiatric and child guidance clinics. Three major trends are visible: one is to recognize the environmental roots of the problems and to explore possibilities for changing community values and institutional organization and to involve youth in these changes. A second is to treat youth where they are to be found, in their everyday setting, through counseling and education. A third is to stimulate young people to help each other and to encourage youth to set up their own organizations for treatment and living.

ADOLESCENTS ARE IN ALL KINDS OF GROUPS

As a result of these trends we find youth on community

boards, police-community relation groups, as offender consultants engaged in correctional reform, as representatives on community-school planning task forces. We find school programs on interpersonal relations, sex and family life education, drug education, drug prevention programs, and also new kinds of recreational programs. In addition, many young people are running free clinics, runaway houses, teenage hotlines, rap sessions. Youth are employed in new careers, in youth-teach-youth programs, in youth patrols and as recreation group leaders. Youth are forming their own communes, or organizing to end the war, reduce discrimination, or improve the environment.

All these efforts draw on and adapt basic small group and institutional theory and practice. This chapter will describe a few examples and discuss the theoretical and practical implications for group treatment.

Each example shows the creation of an opportunity for youth to save others as well as themselves. The programs create respected and responsible roles for youth in which they can exercise initiative. All programs rely on the creation of a positive group climate that gives support to the youth and encourages them to review their feelings about themselves, their values, and their social skills.

YOUTH AS PLANNERS AND CONSULTANTS

An important change over the last few years has been the increase in the proportion of youth in the population. Coupled with a growth of the philosophy that people should have a say in their own destiny, teenagers and young adults have become a powerful pressure group in the community. The reduction of the voting age to eighteen is one example of this. Another is that almost no planning now takes place in regard to youth without youth representatives being included, and not only the conforming and socially approved youth. In the metropolitan county in which I work, youth are included on most endorsing committees, on youth commissions, and on the Mental Health Association Board. They do not yet have representatives on the County Council, hospital board, or school board, but this will no doubt come.

Youth are not only included as planners but they are also employed as consultants and informants. In a recent series of residential workshops in Maryland concerned with law enforcement and correctional reform, offenders were included as consultants and trainers. They participated on equal terms with judges, legislators, lawyers, representatives of important citizen groups, businessmen, administrators and staff of correctional-law enforcement, and social service agencies. The offenders re-lived, psychodramatically, scenes from their own lives that had led them to become serious criminals. They re-enacted prison life, giving the other participants a vivid understanding of the games, stresses, and abuses that occur in every large penal institution. They acted as group leaders and resource members in small and large group discussions, and made recommendations with regard to changes that should be made. They were, of course, supported by trained group leaders, but several showed high talent in group management.

ACCEPTANCE AND UNDERSTANDING LEAD TO CHANGE

These contributions were not only moving and enlightening to the other participants, but they also provided insight and clarification for the offenders themselves. They gained greater understanding of the forces in their own lives that had led them into disaster, and several of them were able to accept more responsibility for their troubles and for the problems in the prisons. These offenders continued as members of a council that was formed out of these workshops and some have since left prison to work in half-way houses, parole and probation work, and drug treatment in the community. There were several vital ingredients in their being able to change: their acceptance as fellow human beings rather than stereotypes by the other participants; their own increased understanding of the stresses and fears of the judges, police, and correctional officers; their increased understanding of the point of view held by victims of crime. The skillful management of these workshops made these changes possible. Many participants, unsure about the nature of the experience, came with considerable reservations. A climate of ambiguity and excitement was fostered, and a number of harrowing and emotional experiences stimulated the desire for change before any planning was initiated. The knowledge and skills required by the professionals included a capacity to plan the workshop, small and large group theory and management, individual dynamics, and a deep understanding of the correctional system.

EIGHT WORKSHOP GROUPS ON DESEGREGATION

Youth representing all the different factions in their schools were included in an eight day workshop to prepare for school desegregation in eight junior and senior high schools. Other members of the workshops included parents, principals, teachers, central office administrators, members of the board of education, and community leaders. Resource consultants were educators, mental health professionals, and architectural students. Eight groups were formed, one for each school, and the whole membership met together in the evening. The students, at first, were diffident in the presence of so much authority. However, they soon took an active, and sometimes prominent part. They were able to present vividly the students' viewpoint and to come up with many constructive suggestions. After a particularly exciting bull session, one of the more conforming students exclaimed, "I had no idea it was permissible to have opinions of one's own that were different from those of parents and teachers!" These students continued to serve as an advisory committee to the principals in planning specific activities. They took part in creating policies, introducing students to their schools, organizing events that improved the climate of the schools and learning to mediate in disputes. They learned to know each other better and to understand and appreciate the customs and problems of different social groups. They learned through practice how to analyze situations and choose among solutions, and to play an important part in changing conditions. As the students were included in the decision making process, and fully respected as individuals having opinions worth listening to, the need to rebel in order to be heard was eliminated, and the urge to acquire status through antisocial activities reduced.

One illustration of how such an approach works took place in a school where interracial conflicts were increasing. At first the school authorities ignored the situation. However, one black girl was always fighting. She was tagged as a behavior problem, adjudged unmanageable, and was under consideration for expulsion. Nevertheless, when the principal decided to set up a task force to explore the conflict in the school, she was elected as one of the representatives of the black students. As she now had a role that allowed her to voice her dissatisfactions, she no longer needed to fight, and she became a constructive member of the school leadership.

In another school desegregation program, black youth

created a sociodrama group to express their feelings and experiences of being black, and their expectations about entering a desegregated school as a small minority. Their skits have been used as a training tool to assist parents, students, teachers, administrators, and community leaders to understand more about the process of desegregation. This group is now adding white students, who had been in majority and minority group situations, and members from other minorities to explore more fully the majority/minority group positions as they had all experienced them. They will also try to use the integration of their own group as a model.

INTERPERSONAL AND SEX EDUCATION IN AND OUT OF THE SCHOOLS

In almost every secondary school workshop today, students request more assistance in learning how to live. They not only want to know how to cope with the practical aspects of modern life, such as care of the home and money management, but they also want to know how to get along with others, how to manage and enjoy sex, how to prepare for marriage and parenthood, and, in general, how to improve the quality of their intimate relations. Their desire for knowledge about sex and boy-girl relationships is so great that even in very large meetings, students will ask such questions as: "How can a girl have sexual relations and be respected?" "How can she avoid having sex and still be popular?" Isn't it true that some girls have babies because they are lonely?" "Does masturbation make you crazy?," etc.

Mental health professionals, school psychologists, and educators have all begun to try dealing with the problem. One school system runs psychology clubs. Several others have instituted programs of family life education that include the physical, social, and biological aspects of heterosexual relationships, marriage, and parenthood. In one particularly interesting out-of-school program, all the teenage boys and girls in a neighborhood with high teenage illegitimacy were invited to explore together every aspect of teenage pregnancy. Meetings consisted of deliberately provocative short lectures and then large and small group discussion. The issues were further deliberated by the boys and girls as they met socially outside the course. The teenagers became much more sophisticated and thoughtful about the consequences of becoming pregnant, and the rate of illegitimate births dropped dramatically. The rate remained low in that neighborhood for the next two years, indicating that the changed value system of the neighborhood group was maintained. However, it gradually rose again as a new generation of teenage leaders had not been exposed to the program.

THE PROBLEM OF THE NEW STUDENT

Because of the mobility of many families, and the changing nature of metropolitan communities today, many teenagers find themselves attending new schools and making new friends almost yearly. In large high schools particularly, it is very easy for students to feel lost and to not know where to turn. Many youth feel lonely and isolated, do not talk easily to parents, teachers, or even to each other, and suffer typical self-conscious confusions of early and middle adolescence.

At a recent teenage convention, fifty minute seminars were held on a wide variety of topics selected by the teenagers. Sensitivity training was a popular choice. Four seminars were conducted on this topic by two leaders. One leader found that while there was a genuine search for information in one session, in another it became clear that the youth really wanted to use the session as a means of getting to know each other better. Introducing exercises, designed for encounter groups, also served to speed the development of an easy relationship. Ice breakers such as moving around and shaking hands, pairing and telling each other something about oneself and then introducing one's partner to the group reduced teenage social embarrassment.

To ease the transition from school to school, some student councils have instituted a buddy system for new arrivals. In other places, homeroom periods have been lengthened, and regular small group discussions have been instituted to deal with current issues affecting the school, or issues of interest to the students. Led by students, the discussions served to train the students in problem analysis and also permitted them to get to know each other and their homeroom teachers better. In one school, a volunteer group of teachers operated a rap room where students who wanted someone to talk to, or had a problem, could spend a study period or lunch hour with an adult who really cared.

YOUTH LED TREATMENT PROGRAMS

It is generally recognized by mental health personnel that those who have experienced problems and found ways to resolve them may well be the most effective helpers for those still struggling with the same kind of difficulties.

In the early sixties, the New Careers program at Howard University started to train school drop-outs for a variety of human service careers. Most of the boys and girls had been in trouble with the law and did not see themselves as successful in legitimate society. Working together in small groups, their views of themselves gradually changed as they learned to work with boys and girls like themselves. One of the youth in a therapeutic neighborhood recreation program failed to meet his group of children who were waiting to go on a trip with him one Saturday morning. The other leaders confronted him with the disappointment the children must have faced and how he had let the whole program down. This boy grew into an exceptionally fine leader and took great pleasure in being able to do something to help the children who were in a spot where he had been before.

A number of schools now employ older boys and girls to tutor younger children who are having some problems in learning. Bloomberg and others have reported that this tutoring program helps the older children, who may have difficulty in their work, to rework basic principles, and gives them a feeling of success and prestige. A recent program in an elementary school set aside one afternoon a week for sixth graders to tutor first and second graders in small groups, thus freeing the teachers for in-service training. The older children met in groups with the teachers of the first grades and discussed their needs and problems. In this way, they learned more about themselves in different roles and gained understanding of how teachers as well as students feel.

GETTING TEENAGERS INVOLVED IN
MENTAL HEALTH HELP

Many teenagers are suspicious of traditional mental health programs today, feeling that they represent the establishment, the family, the court, and the school. Consequently, a wide variety of new treatment resources have sprung up, many of them youth initiated or youth led, with the assistance of one or two dedicated and free thinking adults. A free clinic in one metropolitan area, open one evening a week, provided free medical examination, family planning, VD treatment, individual and group counselling, and a recreation program where youth can play pool, dance, or sit around and chat.

A group of about twelve young teenagers meet three times weekly with a graduate student in psychology and his wife. Sometimes the leaders bring friends and the members sit informally on the floor and deal with whatever is uppermost in their minds; sometimes it is boy-girl relations, other times interracial conflicts, trouble with parents, violence in their neighborhoods, or drugs. Occasionally, they just gossip or discuss some fun they have had. The definition of roles and the contract are different from a classical group psychotherapy session, but not the content and discussion. The youth come to rap of their own accord, and they don't define themselves as needing help or being in trouble. They attend the group only so long as they find it interesting or useful. Initially, there is no commitment to regular attendance. A cohesiveness develops and members show more concern for each other and begin to insist that problems are to be dealt with. As in all young adolescent groups, anxiety is high and there is a tendency to skip back and forth from serious to frivolous discussion, and to leave the room for a while, if pressure becomes too great. The leaders and their friends find they learn a lot about themselves while they assist the younsters in dealing with their problems.

A local hotline employs only high school and college students to man its telephone service. Two or three students work a four hour shift, answering a large number of calls each week. Many calls are from lonely boys and girls. Problems with boy-girl relations and parents are high on the list. However, they also have to deal with harrowing situations such as a youth threatening suicide. Of course, these pro-grams all have professional back-up, but emotions still run high and the teenagers on the hotline have to give each other a lot of support and learn to handle their own feelings, in the process of helping others. For a while, all their demands were made on the organizer of the program, whom they knew well, and they had difficulty using the other professionals who were standing by. Efforts are now being made to really integrate the professionals into the team shifts, so that youth and adults get to know each other well and have confidence in each other.

Two efforts to help young people hooked on drugs employed some of the same principles. In one, a group of young teenagers, who were trying to get rid of the drug habit, enlisted the help of a few adults and formed an information and referral telephone service for those seeking treatment for a drug habit. They instigated a training program that has incidently helped them to understand themselves better, and has now led them to broaden their original focus from drugs to more general human relation problems.

The second involved a recreation program started in a high school delinquency and poverty area by a family service agency. This program was led by a young adult from the area and served about sixty high school students and school drop-outs of high school age. They met evenings, weekends, and vacations, and organized many expeditions and camping trips to broaden their experience. They ran a successful sociodrama group on current youth problems, and presented programs for teenage and adult audiences on the problems of "the street." They developed and manned a number of volunteer activities in human services, in hospitals, old age homes, local recreation, and day care centers for younger children. As time went on, they began to reach out in their schools and neighborhood to other youth they knew who were addicted to hard drugs to try to persuade them to trust their group and leader, and through him to obtain treatment for themselves. The leader, the club members, and the people they served were all involved together in a therapeutic and developmental process. Helping others, the youth learned about themselves, gained skill and experience, and acquired an enhanced sense of self-esteem.

THE GROUP EXPERIENCE IS A COMMON DENOMINATOR

All these programs seek out the strengths in individuals and create opportunities for young people to adopt meaningful roles and increase their skills and self-respect. The programs utilize group methods for support and learning through group interaction and create a self-perpetuating, vast, new source of people who will serve others and develop a society more knowledgeable in human relations.

College Students

MALCOLM L. GARDNER, PH.D.

Though the age range of most college students would place them in the late adolescent classification, it would be of little value to consider them in the framework in which adolescent groups are typically presented and discussed in the literature. College students, for some years, have been waging a reasonably successful fight against the parental philosophy of the college administration, and for recognition as responsible adults both on and off the campus. It is demanded of them that they assert their independence and autonomy while in most instances they are, of necessity, still in an extended state of considerable dependence. At the same time they find it very difficult to identify in any meaningful way with the typical adult group in off-campus adult society. Basically, this is neither something new nor a fad that will pass in due time, but simply the present version of a condition familiar in the past, and one that hopefully will hold for the future.

The environment in which today's college students spend the vast majority of their time bears little resemblance to that from which they came, nor the one to which they will eventually graduate. The only exceptions are those few who establish themselves on campus as on-and-off, part-time perpetual students. If they are eventually in danger of graduating, they change their curriculum and direction in the nick of time and start the whole process over again. Many of these also make up the university therapy population.

PROBLEMS PRODUCED BY THE LARGE UNIVERSITY CAMPUS ENVIRONMENT

Whether the student is on campus to prepare for or escape from the future, the environment of the large university campus impresses itself on both. The students find themselves living in the largest concentration of their own peers, representing the widest variety of backgrounds and values, that they probably have ever had or ever will experience again. And with real estate at a premium, they are ever stacked higher up and closer together. In their campus existence, they are constantly bombarded with the widest variety of new information, ideas, values, philosophies, decisions, and challenges. These reach them from a host of sources beyond their chosen curriculum. As they move from place to place, they are met with handouts, bull horns, bulletins, posters and banners, both mobile and stationary, both low-key and high pressure. They continue to absorb even more from their campus newspapers, magazines, radio, and television stations. The movies, and live drama theaters in their proximity, as well as the campus church of their faith, strive to make their presentations relevant to the campus environment. In addition, the students are also fair game and a ready-made audience for the off-campus society from its noblest to its basest elements. They are on the one hand wooed and praised, and on the other, rejected and condemned.

Most of this environmental experience is deemed essential to a learning atmosphere (and some of it hard won or maintained by a variety of pressures under several banners). Whether they feel ready for it or not, college students must perceive themselves as sufficiently "together" and aware of self to evaluate and meaningfully integrate all of these influences into their own values and goals. For most students, this is an exciting and serious challenge that they meet quite successfully, despite all of their own fears, and the fears and doubts of "that other generation." But for many students the campus environment takes its toll, and they cannot cope without help. They seek help to "get it together" or get their "heads straight." They are confused about "where they are at" and even more, where they want to go. They are not at all sure what is relevant and what is distorted. Distortions are sometimes projected onto the "establishment" or its campus chapter, the university administration. They are striving to understand and gain "independence" and "freedom" in their extended state of dependence and inhibition. They are striving to be open and "let it all hang out" and to communicate and "tell it like it is," while at the same time, fearful of the reaction of others if they dare to do so. On the one hand, they see the value of love and caring, and wish to express these feelings without inhibition, and on the other is their fear of being rejected, ridiculed, or considered "weak." They are in further conflict between values and standards of behavior long accepted as necessary for recognition, and new ones presented to them very convincingly as more meaningful, more exciting, or more free. Behind all of these problems lurk angry and hostile feelings, difficult to cope with, as well as threatening feelings of fear, frustration, confusion, and isolation. Combinations or variations of these problems account for the vast majority of the complaints made by college students seeking professional help.

GROUPS FROM THE CAMPUS POPULATION

Some of these students can and do function quite well in typical community outpatient groups. Most of them seem to benefit more from therapy groups composed *almost* entirely of their peers. Forming these groups produces some practical problems, but it more easily resolves others. The likelihood of people who might previously know each other, meeting again in the therapy group is increased in a group formed from the campus population. The proximity of the students to each other on campus also leads to more out-of-therapy-group relationships and, therefore, a greater incidence of behavior considered to be anti-therapeutic. The extent to which these problems become serious anti-therapy problems varies with different therapists. For some therapy groups, these problems can be damaging, but others can handle them with not too much difficulty.

The varying routines of students and their quarterly or semester changes in class scheduling pose another practical problem, both in forming, as well as maintaining, a therapy group for college students. It is a more acceptable problem in an all student group, than in one composed partly of students. The entire group feels the scheduling to be a common problem that can happen to any one of them and they are motivated as a group to help each other resolve the scheduling conflicts, or, if necessary, find another group meeting time. During student vacations, when they leave the campus and return to their homes in distant cities, or relocate elsewhere, the members who remain behind in the therapy group must give up the therapy sessions as a group or continue without the absent members. Either way, it is possible that disruption can occur in the group process. Usually, some students plan to remain on the near-deserted campus during summer and vacations. They resent any interruption of the group meetings, especially at these times. It is not uncommon for a group of students making their holiday plans to be very concerned about these members of the group, even if the remaining students are in no way seeking this kind of concern or are putting on a brave front. College student therapy groups are likely to take considerable individual and group responsibility for the support of sick members over vacation periods. Not only does their concern relieve the therapist considerably in his work with the more damaged group members, but the incidence of panic phone calls, emergency sessions, and extra drug prescriptions become much less during the vacation periods.

BALANCING A COLLEGE STUDENT GROUP

Obtaining some kind of therapeutic balance in the formation of a student group has a tendency to take care of itself. College students are, by definition, relatively close in age and intellect and tend to distribute fairly well in personality types and problem areas. Schedules, responsibilities, and pressures balance out for male and female students. Socioeconomic, ethnic, and religious differences, if they exist or where they exist, are strongly suppressed by the campus environment, as far as direct confrontation in the group is concerned. Usually, these differences are dealt with intellectually, using as references the coexistence of outside groups, or they are expressed in very subtle ways and subject to immediate denial. The only contraindication for inclusion in a therapy group because of socioeconomic, ethnic, or religious background differences, is the occasional student who is obsessed by varied conflicts in these areas and can only relate to a group of peers who have similar feelings. This kind of student is usually not considered a group therapy candidate in the first place.

Since with few exceptions the identification with being a student is for a relatively short period of time, and student problems arising or intensified by this identification will extend beyond these limits, there is some disadvantage to a group composed entirely of typical college students. The addition of one or perhaps two carefully selected young married members, preferably with children, benefit such a group, by contributing dimensions that go beyond student identification. Recent college graduates, young faculty members, wives of graduate students, or of young faculty members, and similar people seeking therapy, can serve to give the students contact with the outer-campus world that they will be facing soon, by giving them feedback from people identified, to some extent, with both worlds. At the same time, the young adults who live all or a good part of their lives out of the campus environment, gain emotional nutriment and can examine the effectiveness of their own transition from the campus to community life. Students can, of course, reject the "outsiders" by indifference or various forms of overt attack, and the young adults in turn can remain difficult and resistant to the student members. When these reactions occur, the group therapist should examine his selection of the non-student members, or his own handling of the group, in order to determine the best direction to follow toward group cohesion and loyalty.

WHY COLLEGE THERAPY GROUPS ARE UNIQUE

Once formed, the college therapy group can be considered unique in some ways. In the main, college students have considerable knowledge of group functioning and many of them have previously participated in groups of various kinds. Groups with various labels are formed as labs or demonstration exercises in a number of the courses they take. In trying to cope with their own problems, or being "turned on" by the challenge to communicate openly and meaningfully, they seek out and participate in encounter, marathon, human growth, and a variety of other groups that are in plentiful supply on a large campus. Some even have led groups of one kind or another, either as a function of their professional training or because they have experienced groups and feel motivated to pass the experience on to their friends. The students learned group awareness from their academics, and sometimes their considerable knowledge of personality theory, human behavior, and therapeutic approaches, is more detailed than that of the leader. With a group so armed, the therapy leaders can easily find themselves responding to challenges to their qualifications as leaders or their conduct of the group, especially in early meetings. The leaders are drawn into these challenges with questions as to their professional identity and position, as well as having to answer for their theoretical orientation and approach. They might be questioned about theories and therapy approaches unfamiliar to them. Rather than swimming around too long in these challenges, the therapist can usually handle the situation by tactfully placing the challenging member in a position where the challenge must be open and direct rather than indirect and subtle. Despite the element of aggressiveness, it is rare that a group member will make an open and direct challenge to the therapist, but when one does, it is sufficiently threatening to the other group members that they will intervene and even cut it off.

THE THERAPIST HAS LOTS OF HELP BUT LEADERSHIP CAN BE COMPLICATED

A member taking on the role of the leader or acting as an assistant to the leader is a common occurrence in all groups. College students frequently feel particularly equipped to do this with an unusual directness and intensity that is not easy to ignore by either the group or its leaders. It is not at all unusual in college groups for a particular member, sometimes in collusion with one or more other members of the group, to express considerable dissatisfaction with the progress of the group, diagnose its difficulty, propose a solution and some new approaches, and offer to put them into motion. Therapists differ in the variety of techniques they utilize in their groups, and in the degree of freedom they give the group in determining its own approaches. The typical adult patient group more frequently waits for the therapist in one way or another, to indicate or give acceptance to its structure and limits. But the student group can strike against its professional leadership with a suddenness and intensity that can take the leader by surprise, especially in areas where he still has doubts and questions. In such a situation it is easy for a leader to follow the axiom of "when in doubt, do nothing!" With the leader out of it, the other members of the group are more likely to follow the lead of an aggressive, challenging member. This leaves the therapist looking back on the situation after the fact, to determine whether his particular therapy approach or his concept of the group process was appropriate. In such circumstances, therapists can easily find themselves conducting a group that has changed into one not of their choosing, and defending their therapy more to save face than that they believe it to be really therapeutic. It becomes particularly important that one taking on the responsibility of professional leadership of a college student therapy group have a thorough background in group theory and techniques, and sufficient experience to evaluate college students in reference to one's own approach and therapeutic goals.

RESISTANCES OF COLLEGE AGE PATIENTS

Once past the stage of initial leadership problems that may arise, there are all of the usual forms of resistance to the process of therapy. The college student group demonstrates a few resistances that are either of their own unique kind or are used by them more than other groups. For example, this patient population begins group therapy with a greater degree of cohesion in respect to their strong identity as students and their sharing of many common problems. They can easily unite on common campus problems as a diversion from their own personal difficulties, and group discussions can shift to solving the problems of the campus rather than the problems of the group member. Intellectualization is a natural state for the college group, and, in group therapy, it can become a fine art. Even attempts to divert an intellectualization can be turned into an intellectual exercise. College patients have a diverse, colorful vocabulary of labels that they use in an attempt to close the problems off from group therapy discussion, rather than explore them on dynamic levels. The group can divert itself for some time with definitions of a label, complete with hypothetical examples of how it functions, and further definitions of terms utilized in the original definition, and how these new terms operate.

Although classes, extracurricular activities, and work schedules often create practical and justifiable problems for individuals who want to continue in a therapy group, these conflicts can just as easily be manipulated to serve resistance purposes. They serve as excuses for late arrival, early departure, missed sessions, sudden termination of therapy, and sporadic group visits. Practical, justifiable, and convenient, these excuses provide a secondary gain of getting out of difficult work in group therapy. They are too tempting for some students to resist. The student group is usually sensitive to these resistances and will try to cope with them, even to the extent of engaging in a bit of detective work to check out excuses for not being at the group session. It is the leader, however, who has to supply some initiative and direction to the group's attempts at solving this kind of resistance problem.

CAMPUS UNREST IS USED AS RESISTANCE TO TREATMENT

The recent frequency of peaceful demonstrations, and the not so peaceful confrontations and riots on campuses undoubtedly created real problems for some students and brought to the surface material that otherwise might not have been revealed for some time. When they occurred nearby, they were of paramount concern to all of the students, and, of necessity, tended to distract and divert the group temporarily. For some students, these events were used as reasons for therapy resistance behavior that would not otherwise be permitted. The real problems that campus disorders created for some, encouraged others to jump on the bandwagon and gain considerable attention, sympathy, and concern that may not have been therapeutic. School disruptions can serve as a "logical" excuse for a return of previous symptoms and behavior, dropping out of problematical courses, or even dropping out of school or the group. Reactions to these events of our times can be manipulated into mechanisms to divide the group, release anger, and justify attack that otherwise would be deemed inappropriate, or would not be tolerated at all. It is well known that disruptions on campuses are frequently aimed at the administration, and many campus therapists are identified with the administration. If the therapist is not sensitive to this, he can easily find himself manipulated into a defensive or isolated and ineffective position in the group.

INTERACTION, INCLUDING ATTACKS, CAN BE INTENSE

The college student identifies strongly with intelligence, sophistication, and enlightenment, which, in turn, demand that he demonstrate considerable tolerance for a wide range of behavior, values, viewpoints, and human weaknesses. As a result, subject matter that tends to be avoided or approached with considerable difficulty, evasion, and anxiety in other groups, is attacked head-on and pursued in detail by college groups. Their disclaimer of the usual cultural hang-ups gives them the freedom to be intensely critical with the expectation that all confrontation will be accepted constructively. Most college students can not only tolerate criticism and confrontation, but can come back for more and await their turn to dish it out.

Although student groups bring out considerable material and meaningful interactions for therapeutic intervention, the movement of the group as a whole can be disguised. Quite frequently in college groups, after several sessions of this kind of intensity, a member will exclaim "why is it that all we ever seem to do in this group is attack each other?"

Typically, one or two members will immediately move to defend and preserve the way the group has been going, but most of the members will agree that attack is all they seem to do, but *not* all they want to do. Perhaps the best defense is an offense, but in a college therapy group the "offense" can also be an effective resistance. Although college students can tolerate considerable criticism, confrontation, and openness, it is not a safe assumption that all of them are able to show such tolerance. Occasionally, a student will demonstrate not only his ability to take aggressive confrontations, but also will almost masochistically encourage the group to really take him apart. It is only later that the group realizes that that was his last session.

RESISTANCE FOR SOME, HARD WORK ON PROBLEMS FOR OTHERS

All is not difficulty and resistance in college groups! While one member might make use of intellectualization as a defense against therapy, another group member might use it to confront his situation. Where one college student may use schedules as an avoidance of therapy, the others in the group have sufficient information to assess the base of its reality. While the knowledge of group process can be used negatively by some, others can and do use this knowledge to preserve the therapeutic atmosphere with minimal leader intervention. Whereas out-of-group relationships may lead to various complications in the group and to some violations of the group confidence, they are frequently utilized in supportive and constructive ways. When the student members are aware of the need for it, the intensity of criticism and confrontation can be countered with considerable encouragement, acceptance, and support. A contingent of a student group sought out a member on campus who had missed a couple of sessions after a traumatic experience, and brought him back into the group. Other groups have taken a particularly depressed student with them for holidays, or planned among themselves to be sure that his time was filled during the holiday period. They have also taken considerable initiative in drawing an isolated student into social activities, and supporting individual members through temporary crises on much more than the weekly session basis. Older adult group members are known to reach out to peers in trouble but those of college age seem freer in offering such help. The motivation of the campus age group in introducing innovative approaches to various group therapy problems is frequently needed, and timely, and warrants the support of both therapist and group.

NEW MEMBERS ARE FREQUENT

The addition of new members to replace those terminating is usually more frequent in college groups. Fitting into new groups, and adjusting to the addition of new members in existing groups, is a common experience in the campus environment. In most instances, this, along with their shared identity as students, seems to make the introduction of new members into the therapy group a problem the group and the new members handle with little difficulty.

TERMINATION IS FREQUENT

The more frequent termination in college therapy groups results from a variety of circumstances. Dropping out of school and leaving campus goes on at a higher rate among disturbed students. Students well along in the last years of school, but who are seeking therapy, are limited by graduation and end up receiving short-term therapy. Some students are fearful of their parents' discovering their need for treatment and others are equally (or more) afraid of the university administration discovering that they are emotionally disturbed. These fearful students nurture a strong drive for only short-term intervention, since they believe that the longer they go on in treatment, the risk of discovery becomes greater. Like their much older counterparts, college students concede that anyone may need a little help in a temporary crisis, but resist extended therapy as an admission of a weakness they cannot tolerate.

TERMINATION AFFECTS OTHER MEMBERS

The termination of one member sometimes puts in question the continuation of one or more of the other members in the group. For example, two members in a group may depend a great deal on each other, and the departure from the group of one would have a profound effect on the other. In one group, a young woman, ready for termination, resisted and stalled for several weeks, until finally admitting in tears that she continued in the group out of fear that one of the males would run away from treatment if she left. She felt obligated to remain because the group relationship that she worked out with him was instrumental in her improvement but didn't help him as much. Her friend in the group readily admitted that with her announced termination, he had every intention of disappearing back into his previous solitude (where he characteristically turned to suicidal ideation). With this out in the open, the other group members began to help her face termination, and, at the same time, actively support his remaining in the group. Even without such dramatic exposure, the college group is usually quite sensitive to the special relationships within its midst, as it deals with its separation and termination problems.

Sometimes, termination is not really termination in college groups. The other members of the group will check up on the ones they feel terminated unwisely, continue to support them, and even bring them back into the group. Members forced to terminate because they dropped out of school for a period of time, or ran into an impossible schedule problem, or felt the danger of discovery, may request return to the group, and, in most cases, are readily accepted back. When it is known that a break from therapy is temporary, a leave of absence from the group occurs rather than a termination. A place is held in the group for their return, at the end of the "leave." Former members of college groups remain involved in the group after termination in a number of ways. It is easy for them, still on the campus, to continue relationships started within the group, or to run into group members in classes or other areas around the campus. In this way, communication may continue between the group and terminated members for some time after their termination. They satisfy their interest in the progress of members still in the group, and information is conveyed back to the group about their own adjustment.

WHAT ABOUT THE THERAPIST?

The therapist in college group therapy will experience difficulty in avoiding being active and personally involved in the group process. Though the group will generally be quite active without him, they need his intervention and will insist upon his involvement. The leader must be secure in his own intellect, values, and leadership ability if he is to avoid being drawn into unnecessarily defending his attributes. Time after time, the college student group will test his knowledge, needle his values, and challenge his leadership. If he has an identification with the administration, it cannot simply be given up or wished away. If the therapist is sensitive to the emotional needs of the student, identification as part of the administration should not be too much of a problem. The therapist, as a professional person, must have more involvement with the student and his campus life than is acquired by coming from his home to a fully scheduled day at a campus desk, and then returning to his home and community. Going back and forth this way becomes an illusion of campus identity rather than a reality, a fact that students are constantly trying, in many ways, to impress upon the university administration.

The therapist leader also needs to keep in mind the limits imposed by the short-term involvement of various individuals in the group, setting goals and intervening, as necessary, to bring these goals to fruition. Direct, authoritative, and technical sounding interpretations are usually not tolerated at all well by student groups, except in special circumstances. Students are quite sensitive, generally, to being preached to, lectured, or one-upped intellectually by the therapist. At these times they can come forth with varying reactions, from condescending tolerance, to challenge and intellectual diversion, and to openly hostile reactions. During one group session, after a very technical and intellectual interpretation, a female patient stood up and bowed to the therapist with the comment: "Oh tell us more, O great and all-knowing one," to the discomfort of the therapist and great glee of the group.

Setting limits, despite its obvious necessity, is also an area where an authoritative approach is used as a last resort. In almost all instances, the majority of the group is quite sensitive to the need for limits and with a little help from the leader, imposes them very well on themselves. At times they can even get carried away with setting limits, requiring some tempering by the therapist rather than encouragement.

The personal problems of the group therapist can make him quite vulnerable, when working with college student groups. Imitating their dress, appearance, and behavior, when in reality their life style is very different from his own, adds very little, if anything, to the therapist's communication with or relation to the students. Joining in with abandon and enjoying just being "one of the guys" is not necessarily catalytic to a therapeutic process, although it might be a pleasurable experience for the therapist. Taking on the task of straightening out the confused younger generation will result in failure, both in the task and in the therapeutic goals. Enjoying student groups and being stimulated by them is to be desired, but to *need* them to stay young and "with it" is definitely the therapist's problem, and not one for the students to solve for him. Joining the acting-out, resistant, or rebellious behavior patterns of his young patients can do more to unmask the therapist's conflicts than to contribute anything of value to the therapy.

College students bring to the process of a group certain refreshing qualities that make their therapy sessions stimulating, abounding in material for therapeutic interaction, and, they also offer a great potential for satisfying outcomes, both for the student and the therapist.

GROUP THERAPY FOR THE ADOLESCENT

Outpatients

NORMAN S. BRANDES, M.D.

Several years as director of a children's psychiatric in-patient and outpatient unit taught me that not only do young patients suffer from their mental disturbances, but so do most members of their families. This knowledge led me to develop a family orientation to my young patients' problems. Also, it became apparent to me that play therapy and various forms of activity therapy were valuable treatment methods for the child up to twelve or thirteen, but insufficient for the adolescent. Since all adolescents were influenced by the values, limits, and behavior of other adolescents, I developed interest in group psychotherapy, in addition to family therapy, as a way of helping the emotionally disturbed teenager. Group psychotherapy provided a "family-like" setting, as well as interaction with peers under a therapist's supervision.

My first group of adolescents, consisting of four girls and three boys ranging in age from thirteen and one-half to sixteen, met every Saturday morning. All but one had a great deal of difficulty with oral communication. This pointed out that there has to be more than one talker in a good group, especially in an adolescent group.

SILENCES AND ABSENCES PUSH THE THERAPIST TO ACT

In this first group, I sometimes used a blackboard and held a teaching session, making diagrams of family dynamics on the board, and occasionally invited discussion by reading a paragraph from a book on the subject of dependency, sex, or schooling. Regardless of the approach, I spent most of my time and energy in getting each one to talk. When only two or three patients would show up at the session, there was a greater pressure to be active, since young adolescents tolerate silence in therapy with a painful suspiciousness. Despite a few later additions to the group, who were a bit more communicative, the wall of resistance and anxiety still remained high. I spent a great deal of time in the alternate individual sessions with various group members, reassuring them that they should remain in the group. The group was recessed that summer.

In the fall, the selection of adolescent patients represented the same age spread, but the new group was more active and less inhibited. Whenever anxiety provoking subjects, such as sexual experiences, or problems with siblings were raised, there was usually considerable acting out. During such sessions, they would poke one another, wrestle and argue about "who started it." Someone would ask for a cigarette and a pack would go flying across the room without any particular direction. Several times, I attempted to tape a session, but a member would bring a portable radio and play it during the discussions. They tested me repeatedly to see if I would react in an authoritative manner to their infringements, none of which were really that serious. By the end of the year, I discovered that serving soft drinks and candy during the session seemed to break the ice, and at the same time, gave them something to hold onto with their mouths and hands, although this invited some disaster, such as stains on the carpet and furniture.

In the individual sessions, scheduled weekly or bimonthly according to need, we were able to focus on feelings about the rest of the group, as well as why these feelings weren't talked about in the sessions, rather than convincing the individual member to remain in the group, as had happened in the previous year.

AN UNREALISTIC PRESSURE ON THE THERAPIST

After several years of working with adolescent groups, reasons for the heavy sense of responsibility I felt in working with them became apparent. I was expecting myself to represent two significant persons to them—the "perfect therapist" on the one hand, and the human with average, earthlike problems and conflicts on the other. The strain of carrying out this dual expectation left me considerably fatigued after each session. I felt that these youngsters needed an assortment of adult figures with which to identify.

A MULTIDIMENSIONAL PSYCHOTHERAPY APPROACH

Within several years, I began to mix young adults and

older adolescents into my younger adolescent groups. When necessary, family therapy meetings were added to my work with the group members. What went on in each family meeting was discussed in the group sessions with the advance agreement of the young patients involved. Provided that the adolescents didn't object, parents were treated as individual psychotherapy patients. I have found that this kind of multidimensional psychotherapy approach, utilizing various forms of therapy at the same time or in sequence, for more than one member of the family, is expensive and time consuming, but well worth every effort when the results are considered.

YOUNG ADULTS ARE MIXED WITH ADOLESCENTS

In a mixed group, analytic goals were pursued more often, since the anxiety levels produced by analytically oriented group discussion were more easily handled for the group by the young adult patients. Younger patients reached out to and identified with the older ones. The older patients provided a broader psychological matrix for the growth of the younger ones, and, at the same time, they had the opportunity to see the teenage parts of themselves that they had distorted or forgotten.

The therapeutic regimen that I now follow for outpatient adolescent group therapy has evolved over a number of years. The patients that are in my present groups are selected from my own practice. If adolescents or young adults are referred to me for group treatment by another psychotherapist, one of the conditions for bringing them into my groups is that they become my patients, entirely. Interacting with only one therapist avoids confusing transference problems and prevents certain resistances to therapy from coming about, such as the manipulation of the individual therapist and group therapist against each other.

ADOLESCENTS UNDER FIFTEEN

Adolescents under fifteen years do not do well in psychodynamic peer groups that rely chiefly on verbal communication. They seem to do better when individual sessions are combined with alternate family therapy and/or activity groups. In a year or two, if good progress has occurred and the teenager's motivation has survived, then he is introduced into a dynamic peer group. Parents of young adolescents should be told as soon as possible during individual treatment that such a group is planned for the future, to insure their cooperation and support.

SOME CRITERIA USED IN SELECTION

The intelligence, stage of ego development and damage, type of symptoms, previous experience with psychotherapy, as well as religious, educational, and socioeconomic backgrounds are some of the important criteria used in the selection of patients for adolescent group therapy. For example, high average to above average intelligence must be present in order to tolerate the demands of the dynamics of a long-term group. An adolescent with a borderline I.Q., conspicuous immaturity, or limited social experience has no place in a group of bright (but disturbed) adolescents who "have been around." Several years ago, one of my young adult patients had to run to the bathroom to urinate every fifteen minutes, when under emotional stress. He was horrified at the thought of entering a group of peers who would "laugh at him." After several months of individual therapy, he was placed in a middle-aged group in which he was one of two younger patients. Within ten months, he was able to give up both the more protective therapeutic experience of the older group and the weekly individual sessions, and accept changing over into a newly started combined adolescent and young adult group.

Like all group psychotherapies, the more heterogeneous a young people's group is, the better it is, as far as interaction is concerned. Underachievers should be mixed with achievers, quiet patients with fruitful communicators, only children with those from large families, and so on, to achieve maximal communication and learning within the group.

OUTPATIENTS NOT SUITABLE FOR DYNAMIC VERBAL GROUPS

A partial list of those emotional disturbances that should not be treated in dynamic groups that depend on verbal communication of thoughts and feelings are:

(1) Severely withdrawn young patients, incapable of effective communication with anyone, including the therapist.

(2) Psychotic youngsters who are actively hallucinating and experiencing disruptive thought disturbances, including those patients who are taking thought disturbing hallucinogenic drugs and do not agree to stop for the sake of therapy.

(3) Sociopathic and asocial youngsters who cannot apply inner controls to their own behavior. In these cases some type of institutional setting is usually indicated.

(4) Active homosexuals (some therapy groups are capable of tolerating the anxiety caused by an active homosexual if one of his expressed goals of treatment is to become heterosexual).

(5) Emotionally disturbed, retarded, or brain-damaged adolescents who can't keep up with the group's intellectual productions.

MOST OTHER ADOLESCENT DISTURBANCES ARE TREATABLE

Most of the vast array of adolescent anxiety reactions, school disturbances, psychosomatic and psychophysiological illnesses, or adjustment reactions of adolescence are treatable by dynamic group psychotherapy methods.

A WORD ON THE INSTITUTIONAL ADOLESCENT

Although this chapter is oriented to outpatient approaches to group treatment, an informed group psychotherapist should realize that the same clinical principles and treatment philosophy apply to institutional and clinical settings. Realistically, institutions and clinics present more treatment complications, since the group and group therapist must reckon with the extra problems of relationships with multiple hospital and clinic staff, support or lack of support from hospital and clinical administration, the budget of the agency (do you have enough money for coffee, hot chocolate, cake, etc.), and other influences. Sociocultural factors enter into the treatment of institutional and clinic patients a great deal more than with private outpatients. They should be minimized in the group discussions at first, so that the emotional lives of the group members can emerge in the openness of the "hall of mirrors" of the group. Many of these young patients are simply not well enough to cope with these social problems. Others use them as a resistance to dealing with the work of psychotherapy. When the ego strengths of these young patients are strong enough, then all kinds of sociocultural, socioeconomic, and everyday-life-difficulties can be looked at in the group and sometimes, in a very rewarding manner, resolved.

EXPLORE OTHER TREATMENT IF IN DOUBT

When in much doubt about the ability of the young patient to tolerate a group therapy regime, a good rule of thumb to follow is simply to explore other treatment possibilities first. For example, an art group therapy can serve as an excellent bridge to a future para-analytic group experience. A temporary inpatient stay can help to "put it back together" enough for a young patient to tolerate dynamic psychotherapy procedures, including group psychotherapy.

PREPARING THE ADOLESCENT FOR A GROUP

When an adolescent or young adult patient is ready for a group experience, preparation is in order. The information a therapist gives in preparation for entering the group should be framed in a simple and reasonable language. The following is a very simple and abbreviated version of what I try to tell each patient prior to entering a group over a *series* of individual sessions. This structure of information and expectations serves to diminish considerably the anxiety of young patients prior to entering the group.

(1) I can't tell you who is in the group—you'll find out soon enough. They won't know your name or other things about you until after you enter the group.
(2) The reactions of the group members will gradually help to show you how others see you. No one says you have to enjoy this knowledge about yourself. Seeing yourself as others really see you should help you to grow

mentally and become tougher in dealing with emotional problems.

(3) You'll learn things about your fellow group members that will help you to understand others in your world. As a result of this, perhaps you'll learn not to twist around or get mixed up about what other people say and do.

(4) I won't force you to talk about yourself, or your feelings about the others in the group, or about me, but I'll *expect* you to talk. If you remain silent, we'll all try to help you to open up. For example, we'll talk about why you are silent.

(5) The rules are not hard. You must promise to try the group for four or five months. It would not be fair to the others if you came into the group, learned all about who they are and why they are there and then "copped out." You must try to come every time. If you begin to miss sessions, we'll have to talk about that in the group, too. Special mini-groups that would cut out the rest of the group should be avoided, but if you should happen to get over-involved with one or two others in the group, you must agree to talk about it and share the whole experience with the group. It's okay to get angry and express angry feelings but physical expressions of anger like fighting or throwing ashtrays are strictly forbidden. Nobody, including your parents, will know about what goes on in your therapy experience unless you give permission for this information to be disclosed. If your parents call me, you will know about the call.

LENGTH OF TIME AND FREQUENCY

Sessions last from one and one-half to two hours, and are held once a week. At first, individual psychotherapy should contine on a weekly or bimonthly basis and gradually taper down as the need for individual attention becomes less and as the adolescent feels that he is becoming an important person in the group. Young people's groups can continue through the entire summer, but it is difficult to keep a group going on a regular basis when classes are over and vacations and the summer weather start competing. Reducing group meetings to every two or three weeks serves to increase resistance and anxiety in the group. Members, used to meeting every week, complain about the more dilute schedule— that each time it's like "starting over again."

SERVING "GOODIES"

Coffee, hot chocolate, and cake are made available to Saturday morning groups, and soft drinks, hot tea, candy, and cookies to late afternoon groups. Drinking, eating, and serving each other help to "break the ice" at the beginning of the group session. It gives them something to make immediate group communication about and underscores the familial aspects of the group process. It also serves as a vehicle for the stimulation of various transference feelings from time to time. Group members will complain about: "Not enough hot chocolate; Why can't we have more cokes?; You're getting cheap with the cookies and rolls, etc." Sometimes, the complaints mean: "I want you to give more to me!" Often, the behavior over the food and beverages indicates family problems. One day, all the doughnuts were gobbled up and the secretary was asked to go out and purchase another batch. The new sack of doughnuts was taken over by one of the group members who had frequently said that he was never given any real love or attention (except when he was hostile and rebellious) by his mother. He sat on the floor, in front of the coffee table, and one by one, slowly, he took each doughnut out of the sack and placed it carefully on the table, while a discussion went on around him about a member's feelings for the therapist.

THE PARA-ANALYTICAL APPROACH

Adolescents and young adult patients are not content to just "rap" or have emotional confrontations as group therapy unfolds into weeks and months. They need to make sense out of what therapy is doing and where it is going. Ordinarily, they will not accept strict psychoanalytic approaches to their problems because too much resistance, distortion, physical discomfort, and other manifestations of anxiety are stirred up, especially in the younger adolescents, whose egos are still in a state of flux. The para-analytic method of group treatment produces less anxiety than traditional analytic techniques, and it appears to be most productive with these age groups. Para-analytically oriented group sessions allow the psychotherapist the freedom to interpret the present dynamics of the members of the group in terms of the past, and also, in the group session, the therapist is allowed to teach, direct, support, reassure, coax, argue, and be a real person.

GROUP CONSTRUCTIVE FEELINGS

The group psychotherapist must be able to convey, over a period of time, group constructive feelings, such as trust, warmth, and genuine concern, if the group experience is to be truly therapeutic and produce positive changes in the direction of psychological growth. The young members of his group must be taught to share similar feelings with each other, if a para-analytical structure is to hold up over the rigorous test of months and months of therapy, summer recesses, drop-outs, new additions, and other group problems.

Sometimes, adolescent group psychotherapists will become panicky when their groups suddenly diminish in size. Screening and selection for proper balance of the group are bypassed in the therapist's hasty attempts to add patients (usually poorly prepared). Unless very lucky, the group can flounder badly under these circumstances.

The therapist should be ready to add patients when the total number of the group drops to five or six members or less. Although adult groups are capable of having intense sessions with only three or four group members present for a span of many weeks, when an adolescent group suddenly loses four members from a group of eight, group anxiety levels climb too high and it's time to add new patients.

It's best to bring in two or more new adolescent members into an old, continuous group because of the support the new ones can give each other. However, one should be careful not to add four or five new members to a group diminished in size to three or four, since the older ones can react adversely to this invasion and might feel deserted, abandoned, or no longer important. Feeling overwhelmed and out-numbered, their reaction could be one of chronic passivity or hostility, turned against the progress of the group.

Most of the time, the reactions of older group members to a few new additions revolves around a tendency to be quiet and look at the therapist's reaction, or perhaps to over question and therapeutize the new members, in order to give them a good initiation. Sometimes the older members behave this way to please the therapist, other times to show up the new patients. The new patients may sit and be quiet for weeks, and not say anything except after urging and questioning; or, they will be over aggressive in their verbal communication, in an attempt to defy their discomfort and impress the group.

If a group becomes like Grand Central Station, with patients constantly dropping out and new ones added to fill the vacancies, it can't be called a therapy group. It becomes a therapy group only when patients can stay long enough so that self-understanding and some working through of their problems of living come about.

A SMALL GROUP CAN SURVIVE ABSENCES

Occasionally, a cohesive, hard working group of adolescents can survive the absences of many members and still produce significant therapy material. As an example, the following group dialogue concerns only three male patients and myself on a weekend when a rock festival was taking place nearby. That morning four regular members were absent, one male and three females. After about ten minutes of warm-up, the three patients were concerned about a letter and telephone call by Mike K.'s divorced father who moved out west, remarried, and who has been ignoring his son's existence except for occasional presents.

Craig: You told him (Mike K.'s father) about your brother getting busted?

Mike K.:   He's been really upset about that letter. He really didn't understand it at all. He can't take my brother's politics and why he got arrested by the police in that incident.

Mike B.:   Yeh. I was wondering if that was a big thing separating you two, because whenever you start mentioning your family and your real father,

	the world "politics" comes up. It seems like that word always comes in no matter what you say about them, somehow.
Mike K.:	Yeh. Well, I talked to him about politics, but I also talked to him about a list of five things in relationship with him. In general, the relationship with him and my brother, my sister, my relationship with my brother and sister, and I talked about his coming here, and I talked about my going there. I think those were the five things.
Craig:	You wanted him to come here, right?
Mike K.:	Dr. B. wants to see him if he does. I want Dr. B. to meet him.
Craig:	How come you don't want to visit him?
Mike K.:	Well he *wants* me to come there.
Mike B.:	Your father?
Mike K.:	No, the Prime Minister of England!
Mike B.:	There you go again, being hostile!
Mike K.:	I'm sorry, I'm sorry . . .
Craig:	Don't be so sorry. Well, what did you say about your relationship with him?
Mike K.:	In the letter to him I told him I felt he wasn't living up to his part of the deal, that he was shirking his duties.
Craig:	You mean the deal of him being your father? What was the divorce deal, when you were a kid?
Mike K.:	None.
Craig:	There's no deal about him?
Dr. B.:	What do you mean—a deal?
Craig:	I thought there was a written agreement for him to see his father or something like that.

Mike B.: Well maybe that's what he's looking for.

Mike K.: No, no. I'm not looking for a written agreement. You mean, like I want him to write me a letter as an agreement to see me? No!

Mike B.: Well, I mean establishing some relationship by agreement.

Mike K.: Either he wants to see me, or he doesn't want to see me.

Mike B.: Okay, but you want it official, in writing, one way or the other and he hasn't even bothered to answer your letter.

(silence)

Mike B.: A letter from him would make it official and tell you where you stand with him.

Dr. B.: I agree with that, in a way. He's looking for a letter from his father, which he hasn't received yet. He's looked the whole thing over and he's thinking about what he's missed with his real father not being around. He wants his father to make a written agreement about what his duties towards Mike are going to be, or something like that, or, how far he's willing to go in their relationship in the future, or something like that. I hope that Mike's father is going to write that letter. What do the rest of you say about that?

The rest of that particular session established a closeness among these three males that lasted through some trying therapy moments. Often, the three brought the group together in a cohesive strength to face and resolve problems that were threatening and overwhelming.

Somewhere in the cortex of the group psychotherapist,
there should be an organized pattern of goals for these
stormy adolescents and troubled young adults. It helps to
consider these very important goals as having immediate,
intermediate, and long-term potentials, and that some goals
might have to be postponed, others achieved earlier, and
some, perhaps, even dropped.

IMMEDIATE GOALS

Four immediate goals are necessary in order for the
patient to be reached by group therapy at all. The young
group members have to (1) understand the basic ideas of
what group therapy is all about; (2) accept the therapist's
and group's expectations of them upon entering and being
in the group; (3) gain some kind of relief from distracting
symptoms, such as depression, frightening and painful psychophysiological anxieties, or suicidal preoccupation; and,
(4) keep up the motivation to deal with the discomfort of
coming into a group of strangers and "getting close" with
them. Some patients have as difficult a time with the physical closeness of sitting next to the others, as the psychological "closeness."

In my experience, group psychotherapy, alone, is not
enough to help most young patients accomplish these goals
unless they have had a substantial exposure to individual
psychotherapy. A schedule of individual psychotherapy sessions should be kept up from the beginning and, in most
cases, should occur weekly, during the working through of
these initial goals of group treatment. The duration of time

needed to achieve these initial goals varies significantly from adolescent to adolescent.

INTERMEDIATE GOALS

The two intermediate goals are on a higher level and more difficult to attain, yet are just as important for the continuation of therapy. The "communication of intimacies" is not as easy as it sounds and requires a lot of therapy work. It means the patients have to acquire a relatively easy, spontaneous, not too guarded way of sharing intimacies about themselves with each other in relation to all others in their world, both inside and outside the therapy group. Some examples would be talking about masturbatory habits, revealing unusual fears (like one very attractive female adolescent's fear of the presence of sharks in public or private swimming pools), homosexual anxieties and contacts, or a history of incestual experiences, just to name a very few.

Only after intimacies are shared can the other intermediate goal, the acquiring of a more honest self-evaluation and so-called insight, be achieved. Unlike individual psychotherapy, the self-understanding that evolves in group psychotherapy comes, for the most part, from interactions with the other group members, and not just the therapist. Learning how to face yourself as others see you in the group can be a painful experience. The group therapist must see to it that the rest of the group doesn't offer distortions rather than truth, and at the same time, he must help to prevent the "taking and dishing it out" process from being too painful. It is necessary to go over "insights" more than just a few times, as the group goes on, in order for them to be absorbed into the self-concepts of the various group members. College-agers, especially, intellectualize the understanding and acceptance of insight and may resent repetition of facts and interpretations about themselves in the group, as a resistance to making lasting changes.

RESPONSIBILITY IS A LATE GOAL

Late group therapy goals are reachable after the therapist has explored all avenues with the patient as well the rest of his family (using as much of a multidimensional approach as is necessary and practical). These goals are bound up with the freedom to grow and reach psychosexual maturity, a relative state of well-being, and a feeling of responsibility for self and others. Sometimes, because of the need to achieve a "sense of responsibility," the alliance between adolescent and therapist is an unhappy one. At the same time, the facing up to responsibility for himself, that is, responsibility for what he says, what he does, and what becomes of him, becomes a goal accepted and attainable by the young patient in the last stages of therapy. At this point, he trades projection for responsibility. If this goal is reached, then he is encouraged to assume a sense of responsibility for other group members and then, gradually, for those people that are close to him outside of his therapy group. At this point, the patient is able to function as an autonomous being, yet reasonably comfortable in accepting the dependency of others as well as being dependent on others.

During the final period of a long-term group experience, the group therapist cannot be inactive in dealing with the resistance of his young patients to being responsible for themselves and others in the group. He must remind, suggest, interpret, ask for interaction, and create conditions for emotional involvement with others. To be on their own in a relatively independent state of being, comfortable in being dependent when necessary, and then being independent once again, is a welcome reward for young patients after a lot of hard work in therapy.

Family Therapy

ERNEST E. ANDREWS, M.S.W.

$\mathbf{A}$ consideration of therapeutic work with adolescents at the level of family intervention brings up several basic and general assumptions about the nature of adolescence, the nature of family, and the relationship between the two. One way to view the family is as a human system that undergoes a life cycle of two constantly alternating processes: (1) being together for the sake of support and emotional nurturance, in order to promote confidence, security, and self-esteem, and, on the other hand, (2) being apart for the sake of autonomy and growth, in order to put one's reality skills to the test of functional and independent responsibility. The onset of adolescence in a member of a family brings forth a critical and crucial time when both of these processes come into play. Adolescence is the beginning of maximum autonomous separation from the family and of independent growth. It is also the time of ambivalent dependency during which support and nurturance are necessary. The family may be seen as the crucible of autonomy and growth as well as the reservoir of support and nurturance for the adolescent. When the adolescent transacts with his family members, especially the parents, he often helps them to understand the unresolved, pressing, and latent need for his autonomy and growth, as well as his need for support and nurturance.

FAMILY CENTERED THERAPY

Therapeutic management of the adolescent at the level of family intervention assumes, therefore, that the other members of the family are deeply involved in both the autonomy and the nurturance of the adolescent, and can be of considerable help to him. Essentially two forms of "family therapy" have been utilized with adolescents. In the *family centered therapy* approach, there is a recognition of the family as emotional and nurturant, with the members of the family seen separately or in pairs but not as a total unit. This approach maximizes the separateness of the adolescent from the family. In my experience, this approach has a tendency to weaken the supportive and nurturant aspects. At times, when lack of support and nurturance is characteristic of a family, the family centered approach is more advantageous than a family systems therapy approach.

FAMILY SYSTEMS THERAPY

The *family systems therapy* approach treats the family

as a human transactional system in distress. The adolescent, as an interlocking and emotional unit, manifests through his symptoms the symbolic distress of the family. The family, as a group, is the unit of therapeutic attention. The family systems therapy approach maximizes any support and nurturance existing within the family. Autonomy and growth of the adolescent is very difficult without this support and nurturance, and it is next to impossible for the adolescent to be supportive and nurturant to others unless the family functions in this way. The family systems therapy approach is the main concern of this chapter.

SUPPORTING THE ADOLESCENT'S SEPARATION AND READJUSTMENT

Both the principal and the primary tactical advantage of family therapy is to help the separation of the adolescent from primary relationships within the family and to readjust his relationships outside the family, while maintaining a positively supportive familial relationship. Up until the teen years, the concentration of therapy is primarily upon reintegration of the child into the primary relationship system, rather than separation from it. The therapeutic task with an adolescent in the family is to see who is able to let go of whom within the family, and, at the same time, to allow growth and autonomy without withdrawing support. This is the essential task of the adolescent and his family if they are to survive one another, and it becomes the essential task of the therapist.

A COMPARISON OF FAMILY AND NON-FAMILY GROUPS

While family therapy has the distinct advantage of allowing the therapist to deal directly with the nature and consequences of a patterned system of relationships, it also presents a therapeutic challenge in the form of intense resistance to change. The therapist not only finds a useful, tactical advantage in dealing directly with the family, but he also assumes a "package deal" that contains some significant disadvantages. A comparison between family therapy and non-family therapy groups makes readily apparent the rather pervasive nature and extent of these disadvantages. In the first place, each family is a "natural reality" group, in that it has a group reality existing outside of therapy. Family members have relationships with one another before coming to therapy, during the therapy sessions, between therapy sessions, and will most likely continue to have relationships after therapy has been concluded. The therapy group, composed of individuals who are not related to one another, has a reality only during the group therapy itself, and does not usually exist outside of therapy.

This contrast between the family therapy group as a "natural reality" group and the non-family group as a "created reality" group has the general consequence that the members of the family are in control when it comes to matters of who is in the family, and what the nature of their relationship is to be. The therapist has no choice as to who is in the whole family group and he is, by definition, an outsider acting as a helping professional. Despite the need for his help, he is also seen as a threat and an intruder to their established dysfunctional pattern. In the non-family therapy group, the therapist selects the patients and, in fact, can select them in order to provide for a level of emotionality in the group that is productive of both substantial emotional support and awareness-provoking interaction.

In the family group, emotional support is often appreciably diminished, and, in fact, this lack of nurturant quality among the family members is one of the principal reasons why symptoms develop within the family. On the other hand, in a non-family therapy group, emotional support is extensive and generally helps the patient to accept and make use of the confronting and interpreting that goes on. The family group is unconfrontative except in an accusatory or deprecatory way, and the family members often cover up rather than reveal what they are really doing. The fact that the adolescent is either in the process of fighting against or clinging to his familial dependency, autonomy or support, makes him both half in and half out of the family. This makes him a valuable person in family therapy, since he lives within his family's system, but is in the process of removing himself from it. For this reason, the therapist can utilize the adolescent's capability of removing himself, somewhat, from the resistance of the family.

THREE LEVELS OF FAMILY THERAPY WITH ADOLESCENTS

Crisis Intervention is an "incident focused" initial approach necessitated by a chronic emotional disturbance within the family that has suddenly been acted out by the adolescent. The acting out is in a form of behavior that is either disrupting to normal family routine or considered antisocial within the community. The parents bring the adolescent to the therapist as the "problem" and all in the family are only interested in resolving the current "unacceptable behavior." Once the family's uncomfortableness that has been prompted by the adolescent's acting out has subsided, the family may decide not to continue in therapy with the adolescent; they have accomplished what they came in for and will terminate further contact.

The crisis perceived by the family with an adolescent typically involves: (1) angry and hostile scenes ranging all the way from loud shouting matches to physical assault and property damage, either within the home, on the front porch, or in the street (adolescents are certainly not unaware of the tactical advantages of showing the neighbors as well as the family the full extent of their resentment and frustration); (2) hysterical episodes, ranging all the way from guilt inducing threats like "you'll be sorry" to outright suicidal gestures and behavior; (3) the sudden discovery of adolescent drug use ranging from the purely accidental discovery to the openly staged and contrived, to purposely upset the parents; (4) sexual acting out goes all the way from easily discovered "hot" letters, to the sudden announcement of an impending pregnancy, and; (5) runaway episodes ranging from the relatively well-planned and announced to completely impulsive escapes.

When Sally, an only child, came in with her parents, the principle concern of the parents, but not of Sally, was their daughter's impudent and provocative behavior in school, for which she had been dismissed. A prior phone conversation with the father, however, made it clear that his real concern was Sally's sexual experiences with some boys, involving fellatio and group masturbation. The early sessions with Sally and her parents were marked by a parental concern over school issues with not a mention of the sexual behavior. This concern about school made Sally angry and she talked about her parents avoiding the real issues. It soon became apparent that the parents had various intimacy difficulties that revealed themselves to be in an unsatisfying sexual relationship. The father, unconscious of himself, but certainly not of Sally, turned to her with rather seductive interests, leading Sally to an almost panic stricken state of anxiety that she expressed outside of the family with her sexual behavior. During the sessions, mother and daughter were in an intensive competitive relationship in which the mother, at times, treated Sally either with outright hostility or depressed withdrawal. Therapy drew attention to the affectional relatedness of the parents rather than their problem of sexuality so that Sally's presence was helpful as a reality assessor. Sally's anxiety diminished as she was able to view the parents' relatedness rather than the ambush and guerilla tactics of the past. The case of Sally and her family is an instance of an initial symptomatic crisis that led to family therapy, which, in turn, uncovered a more chronic underlying problem.

WHAT IS THE CHRONIC UNDERLYING DISTURBANCE?

In crisis situations, it is imperative for the therapist, the adolescent, and his family to evaluate how much of a chronic underlying situation has been made manifest by the current crisis. If the adolescent and his family can begin to think of a resolution of this fundamental disturbance within the family, the adolescent may emancipate himself and grow into responsible autonomy in a secure way. He may be able to leave his family with a feeling of self-confidence, and an appreciation and concern for his parents, rather than carry with him into adulthood the residue of traumatic anger, distrust, and frustration that is so often most difficult to work through in the therapy of adults.

INTERGENERATIONAL CONFLICT: WHO IS RESPONSIBLE FOR WHO'S AUTONOMY?

A second level of intervention deals with *Intergenera-*

tional Conflict, which can escalate into an anxiety ridden intergenerational war within the family, with much bitterness, rancor, vindictiveness, retaliation, and unnecessary punitiveness. Family therapy intervention at this intergenerational level is very much concerned with the fourteen to eighteen year old adolescent who is still maintained in the family within a parent-child relationship. A therapy question that comes up is "who is responsible for who's autonomy?" Families often view the conflict as a chronic situation of several years duration that has been of great concern to all and has not yielded to any resolution efforts. As time passes, there has been a gradual escalation of conflict. This pattern may be broken with runaway episodes if the conflict becomes acute enough.

There are times when the parents of a fourteen to eighteen year old adolescent realize that control over the "child's" right to be himself is either a basic need for confirmation of their own identities or an autonomy and control conflict that has been repressed in the marital relationship, but rearoused by their adolescent's strivings. Therapy would concentrate on the process of emerging autonomy and on defining the nature and direction of support and guidance between adolescent and parent. Rather than get caught up in the content of "who is to decide what," therapy must move into the area of "who is doing what to whom with what painful consequences." Underlying many of these intergenerational conflict situations is a marital relationship in which there is no success in controlling the spouse, so that attempts are made to control the adolescent children.

FROM PARENT-CHILD TO ADULT-ADULT

A third level of therapy with the adolescent and his

family, the *Separation* and *Family Reconstruction Level,*
deals with the eighteen to twenty-two year old late adolescent. Whether one accepts the distinction of the later years
of this age group representing a stage of "youth" rather
than adolescence, the emphasis is essentially for both the
adolescent and the family to relinquish the parent-child relationship and replace it with an adult-adult relationship.
Of course, there will still be a generation gap, but a gap that
represents a younger adult generation and an older adult
generation. Not only is it necessary for the adolescent to separate from his family but it is also necessary for the family
to reconstruct itself around the removal of one of its members from the family's support and nurturing relationships.

If the adolescent is not able to separate and re-establish
support within his peer relationships, he will experience
great difficulties in forming a mutually satisfying marriage
and family of his own. If he keeps returning to his own
family for support and nurture, these qualities in his own
marriage and family will become diminished, if not negated.

LEAVING THE FAMILY

Individual and group therapy are often used together
with family therapy to enhance the adolescent's opportunity
for autonomy and differentiation from his family. The adolescent cannot really leave his family if the separation occurs
with bitterness over unresolved dependency and autonomy
issues. He must be able to develop aspects of his own identity outside of his family, with other adults as well as with
his peers. The use of both individual and group therapy,
along with family therapy, offers an ideal combination of
therapies to help bring about realization of his identity.

Ralph, age 19, was referred to me with his parents for
a family evaluation. The referring therapist knew that the

parents were interferring with Ralph's attempts at decision-making from his discussions in his therapy group. Ralph had an older brother, 21 year-old Eddie, who also came in with the family. Eddie had seldom been out of his room since graduation from high school and often did not get out of bed in the course of the day, frequently roaming about the home late at night. The situation was somewhat similar to Ralph's who was expelled from a very liberal college for failing to show up for class and hand in written work because he also seemed to be glued to the sack. The parents seemed passive and dependent, indecisive and remote. As youngsters, these boys had literally not been permitted out of the yard until they entered kindergarten at age five.

During an early interview Eddie muttered to himself and made tic and other peculiar gestures, while Ralph tended to be sardonic and angry. It became apparent that any attempt by the boys to leave their parents and assume responsibility for their own lives met with the parents' extreme ambivalence. The opportunity for responsibility was given without support to assume the responsibility. The parents engaged in active criticism of the boys' attempts at emancipation. Their behavior was overprotective and manipulative with regard to their sons' attempts for independence. They expressed a great concern over their togetherness as a pair if the boys were to leave them. In actuality, the marital relationship was characterized by a mutual remoteness with little emotional satisfaction. Eventually, the parents were able to set a date for Ralph's leaving home and assuming responsibility for himself. Strengthened by his experience in family therapy, as well as individual group therapy, Ralph was able to pack his suitcase three days prior to this deadline and leave pleasantly, moving some eight states away. He kept up a periodic, although not extensive, phone correspondence with the family through which it became apparent that he was developing his own life style.

FAMILY THERAPY TECHNIQUES

The various techniques of family therapy can be broken up into four basic sequences.

(1) *Analysis of Communication.* This process is of primary significance in that it helps the family as well as the therapist to define the provocation and retaliation pattern that is so characteristic of families with upset adolescents. It is necessary for the therapist to help the family members communicate by helping them to complete messages, complete meaning, and listen to the other. Most of the communication in dysfunctional families is either incomplete or indirect and carries an effect of latent threat or hostility. The end product is a variety of nonverbal messages such as sulking, avoiding, and other pain-evasive devices that signal "keep away" rather than "here's what I need."

In the early sessions with Sally and her parents, she would constantly interrupt any emerging communication between her parents for fear it would escalate into damaging conflict. It was interesting to note that the parents seemed to expect and perhaps had even counted on this kind of intrusion from Sally to perpetuate the alienation between the two of them. The parents' focus would then quickly shift back onto Sally until the therapist said repeatedly and firmly, "Sally, we take the time to sit and listen to *you*—and I expect that you will be fair enough to do the same for your parents! If there is some trouble between the two of them, I'm going to help them with that." Inherant in this therapy process is both the prevention of disruption and a meaningful, supportive gesture to manage the conflict, rather than allowing it to "destroy" the relationships under scrutiny.

(2) *Clarification of who was doing what to whom.* This is the natural outgrowth of the analysis of the communication sequences of family therapy. It transfers communication to the realm of interpersonal reactions. The therapist must shift the family away from blame and fault, to who is responsible for what. This shift has considerable importance for producing lasting change in intrafamilial relationships. The adolescent frequently identifies himself as a victim only and not as a contributor to family dysfunction. Therapists often make the same mistake if they do not view the dysfunction in terms of the total family.

(3) *Revelation of critical emotional needs.* When the provocative and disruptive processes in the family have been slowed down by the therapist, they can be viewed by the family as realistic sources of unhappiness and disturbance with one another. Then it becomes possible to look at the critical unmet emotional needs among family members. Often an unresolved marital problem, such as jealously, becomes manifest when the adolescent plays one parent against the other for his own narcissistic gratification. As a result, emotional support within the family can be diminished in part, and the family may become oriented toward manipulation rather than negotiation. Each family member may react with: "get what you can, in any way you can, because nobody will *give* without strings attached." If the parents are too jealous or competitive to give affection and support to one another, they cannot give to their children.

(4) *Methods of negotiated and mutual need satisfactions.* These methods ask who is willing to do what to promote a better outcome. "What are you willing to do that would help things to turn out differently?" The family is asked to negotiate a pattern of more satisfying family interaction, which will include the adolescent realizing a significant degree of autonomy.

As this phase of family therapy is worked through, most therapists report multiple kinds of acting out behavior, not only from the adolescent, but also from the parents. The parents demonstrate this either through demands and threats or blackmail tactics, which arouse the adolescent to angry outbursts. If the therapist does not exercise a firm and directive stance with both the adolescent and his family at this point, the therapy may disintegrate into a series of emotional binges that are destructive to healthy outcomes. Emergent behavior can best be dealt with as it is happening during the session itself and not by encouraging and responding to anecdotal reports. After-the-fact reporting only leads to hindsight or second guessing as to what really happened, since the therapist was not actually there. This may lead to demands for "immediate sure-fire solutions" as a substitute for negotiated, gradually emergent solutions.

USEFUL PSYCHODRAMATIC ROLE PLAYING TECHNIQUES

Because of the heightened emotional intensity of family transactions that involve an adolescent, there are several psychodramatic role play techniques that may be useful in the family sessions and can be of advantage in promoting awareness.

(1) *Role reversal*: A father and son can assume the behavioral stance that the other each typically takes and continue to attempt to communicate with one another with this role reversal in play. The other members of the family, along with the therapist, act as observers to validate the authenticity of the role re-enactment. This kind of psychodramatic experience can help the family members view themselves through the mechanism of the role reversal as a rather difficult person to deal with and each may develop

an awareness of how it must be for the other person as a recipient of their behavior.

(2) *Avoider-seeker Exchanges* by prescription, in which family pairs are told to specifically assume either avoider or seeker postures in obtaining meaningful emotional contact with each other.

An example would be the relationship between Carl and his father, who both expressed some concern and anger over their lack of closeness and friendly communication. During the interviews it was observed that both were flat in their emotional responses. Carl would make feeble overtures to his father who, unsure of his intent, acted as though he were unaware of the boy's attempt to make contact with him. The therapist suggested that Carl and his father face one another and directed Carl to actively seek some information from his father. They were instructed that no matter how vigorously Carl sought information, his father should not give it. This re-enactment of a characteristic way in which they related to each other was reversed in a little while, and Carl became the seeker. Relating as "the other one" elicits significant feelings from persons who are inhibited or who are denying their feelings. Each may begin to see his contribution to a disturbing outcome, rather than accusing the other of a wrongful relationship.

Psychodrama and role playing certainly should not be used as a substitute for what the family must eventually do in any case—develop insight and need-satisfaction. Once there is awareness of how each provokes, disturbs, avoids, and incites predictable responses from another in the family, decisions can be made to avoid these patterns of behavior and adopt more healthy ones.

Psychodramatic techniques are useful only after the therapist establishes a relationship with the family that helps the parents and children see his participation in the intrafamilial behavior as a positive contribution to their family life. The techniques should be entrusted to experienced therapists whose judgement and sense of clinical timing incorporate these methods in a productive and meaningful way, rather than as resources in time of dire desperation.

MULTIFAMILY GROUPS

The family therapist needs to be flexible in order to deal with severe resistances. Multifamily groups, composed of three families, who may meet for either a minimum of two hours a session each week or may come together for periodic day long marathons for eight to twelve hours, are sometimes helpful when family therapy is at an impasse. The selection of families for these multifamily groups should be done with the same care and consideration as the therapist uses in selecting patients for any heterogeneous "classical" therapy group, paying particular attention to the balance of emotionality in terms of aggressivity and passivity.

DAY-LONG FAMILY SESSIONS

Temporarily, the family therapist may elect to meet with a resistant family on a day-long rather than weekly basis. A day-long, eight to twelve hour "mini-marathon" for a single family can be a rewarding experience and help break through high resistance areas. It seems natural for families to accept this treatment approach, since they live together. It is living together in a more satisfying manner that is the underlying motivation to remain in family therapy.

EFFECTIVENESS

Family therapy sessions give the opportunity to evaluate symptoms that disguise deeper feelings of concern, anxiety, anger, and threat. When the level of emotionality is controlled and subdued, family relating can be direct and genuine, without inhibition by symtomatic ploys and interpersonal games.

It is interesting to contrast how the adolescent describes his parents in relation to him, and how, in fact, they actually relate to him during the family therapy session. The dreadful descriptions of many parents would lead one to presume that the adolescent could very well plunge into the depths of hell unless a miracle occurred. This initial image usually fades away in the presence of the adolescent and his relatedness to his parents during therapy. The discrepancy between images and real persons in the family can be so great that it almost has a delusional quality. Some of the things family members do to one another and the manner in which they perceive one another sometimes resembles insanity.

Family therapy gives the therapist an opportunity to disrupt provocative transactions that perpetuate negative self-esteem outcome. The interventions of the therapist must be active, aggressive, and often blunt, in order to bring about this disruption, avoid appearing to condone the family dysfunction, and seize the opportunity for immediate learning and reinforcement.

Another advantage of family interviews is the ability of both the therapist and the family to directly view and to openly deal with all kinds of alignments and splits that diminish family support and keep persons apart from one another. The schizms and political power tactics in the family system can be noted and challenged, and alteration can be attempted within the context of the interview itself.

The kinds of symptoms chosen by family members, and "who ends up with what symptom," and, more particularly, how a member of the family becomes identified as *the* patient and is labeled as *the* symptom bearer, is more understandable when the social content of family relatedness is viewed directly by the therapist. Often, therapy reveals that all members of the family have symptoms and they coalesce into a pattern that perpetuates the sick family and destroys interpersonal meaning and psychological survival.

Finally, the patterns of actual reciprocal communication and the consequences of such are viewable and manageable within the context of the total family. To have the members of the family each comment alone, outside of the presence of the others, as to what is occurring in the relationship, can result in an incomplete and one-sided picture. The withdrawn husband married to the bitchy wife is not essentially a description of fault and blame in the failure of human relatedness, but is much more fundamentally a description of an interpersonal reciprocity in which the more she bitches, the more he withdraws, so the more she will bitch and the further he will withdraw. This process will reciprocally escalate, until disrupted by either participant or the therapist. This kind of phenomenon is one of the most basic perpetuating mechanisms of family dysfunction and symptoms.

SOME CONTRAINDICATIONS

All family problems with adolescents are not indications for family therapy. Family sessions can escalate and enhance symptoms of despair in a family exhibiting deep hostility and acting out, especially if family controls of emotionality are poor. The intervention of family sessions also becomes a disadvantage when a family is on the verge of multiple separation due to family disintegration. The decision by family members to live apart has, itself, diminished intensely negative, effective interactions, which can only be reinstated by family sessions. Finally, when severe and distinctly opposing alignments exist within the family, family sessions are ill-advised and can bring these conflicts into the open with increased intensity. In these instances, a therapist would need to consider individual or non-family group therapy instead of, or in preparation for, family therapy.

THREE WAYS TO USE FAMILY THERAPY

When the needs of the family indicate that family therapy is the treatment of choice, the chief concern must be with the family dysfunction. However, once the dysfunction is alleviated, certain family members may be referred for individual or group psychotherapy. This was not possible before, due to the interference of overwhelming family conflicts. Family therapy, then, can be a connecting link from one phase of psychotherapy to another. Sometimes, it is the well-timed intervention of family therapy that provides the understanding and support necessary to keep a patient going in individual or group psychotherapy. Family therapy offers a wide spectrum of treatment possibilities as well as rewarding opportunities for the mental health of adolescents.

Transference—Countertransference

FERN J. AZIMA, PH.D.

Transference as a group phenomenon is a matter of great debate today. As is well-known, group therapists differ widely in the use of the concept. The "orthodox" make it the cornerstone of treatment and the "revolutionaries" have cast the term out. In fact, it is probably fair to say that presently the countertransference of the therapist is more "legal" to discuss than the transference feelings of the patients.

A DEFINITION OF TRANSFERENCE

The modifications of the concept of transference appear linked to the increased focus on differing anthropological data from other societies, the shift to Freudian ego psychology, modifications by the Neo-Freudians, the impact of Kurt Lewin, and the last decade's increasing concern with the group's "interaction" and "existence," broadening the transference concept to the wide panorama of today's encounter techniques. We are concerned only with this rapid historical tracing of the forces that caused mutations of the transference concept. The more detailed definitions can be pursued by the interested reader elsewhere.

Tranference in this chapter on adolescent group psychotherapy will be taken to signify the wide array of repetitive or emotionally significant manifestations of patient behavior in relation to the therapist, other group members, and the group as a whole. From this point of view, transference is to be considered as stretching horizontally in the present, vertically in time, and integrating both intrapsychic and interpersonal phenomena. At times, transference may be considered diluted by the presence of others in a group and, at other times, the concensus of the members of a group magnify its intensity. The "essence" of transference in a group is different from its appearance in the one-to-one setting. By adding a third listening member, or a sixth or seventh, the reflective attitudes of reciprocating patient and leader are altered. Both therapist and member must be continually alert to the possibility of response to another member and, therefore, each "set" is continually monitored and cannot be maintained as rigorously as in a diadic or one-to-one setting. The individual patients have to trust and accept the decision of the group as well as the group therapist in an interpretation of transference and then therapeutic work can begin to modify transference behavior that may be diluting the effect of therapy. This author prefers to expose and work through repetitive distorted communication patterns in the group process, which, in turn, allow the emergence of new kinds of interaction and learning about others.

Here, countertransference is defined as the therapist's subjective, emotional, or conflictual response to an individual patient or to the pressures of the group as a whole. It is a myth to consider that any therapist can escape manifestations of countertransference reactions. If the leader's irrational responses become overabundant, his therapeutic function is destroyed and this will often lead to the destruction of the group. The issue for the therapist is how to diminish his own "distorted" reactions, and, at the same time, help the patients understand and resolve problems. At times, the therapist can become aware of his feelings of inappropriateness, anxiety, hostility, fearfulness, or seductiveness. Sometimes, the group members identify and discuss this behavior in their leader. Watching behind a one-way screen has a great advantage for peer-therapists and residents in training, who can question the motives of verbal or nonverbal behavior in the leader, to which the leader may be "blind."

Today's group therapists are less fearful of expressing themselves and are therefore more active and involved in the group interaction. The classical dictum was for the therapist to maintain a neutral mask of anonymity in order that his feelings not disturb or displace the projections of other participants. Now, the therapist's own style largely governs the degree to which he participates. There is no state of absolute neutrality for the therapist and even the most benign, benevolent individual communicates many nonverbal cues that identify his accepting or rejecting attitudes toward the material being presented. No matter what the personality of the leader, the skill and experience that allow him to relate, think, and treat distorted patterns of communication become essential. If the leader's conduct is no more rational or "normal" than the group members, then, in this author's framework, a "therapy" group is not possible.

Younger adolescents have more difficulty in verbalizing and conceptualizing, and, in large measure, depend on nonverbal channels of working through more of their problems. In the main, the bulk of the author's experience has been with groups of boys and girls, ages fifteen to eighteen, with diverse symptomatology, low-average to superior intelligence, and in the lower and middle socioeconomic range. When deciding on the composition of these adolescent groups, I seek to attain a balance between the acting-out character disorders and the neuroses.

AN ADOLESCENT GROUP

This out-patient, clinic, adolescent group was conducted behind a one-way mirror in a training program for psychiatric residents and staff. The sessions were held weekly, for eighty minutes, beginning in October and continuing through the end of June. Two or three members were usually carried into a second year's treatment in a new group formation. It was the only type of therapy they recieved. The therapist interviewed each member to evaluate his candidacy for the group. The "rules" that were established are the following: (1) that the therapist is prepared to deal only with issues brought out in the group. Private phone calls are not taken unless a true crisis emerges. Letters are brought to the group unopened. (2) The members are asked to inform their parents that if questions arise, the questions will be answered by the social workers in the clinic. (3) The therapist makes it very clear that confidentiality between members and therapist is strictly enforced and that if parents or agencies "leak" information this in turn will be passed onto the members. In effect, the message is clear that if parent or agency need to call, the patient must be informed. Initial sessions are punctuated with discussions of the operating procedures.

GROUP THERAPY : FREEDOM, NOT LICENSE

In the early stages, the therapist (the author) acts as an active, outgoing, positive individual who guarantees freedom of speech. She quickly states that the group is a forum for discussion and not for physical acting out. The "rules" define the limits and parameters and probably prevent wild acting out that occurs when no controls are provided. Within this framework, an atmosphere of safety that encourages frank discussion is provided.

The theoretical framework practiced by the therapist integrates a modified, psychoanalytically oriented approach with interaction and group process, stressing a psychosocial analysis of interpersonal communications. It is a schema that has formed over time, working within a multidisciplinary framework. Intrapsychic data is always considered in reference to its manifestation within the social field. The present coping style of each individual adapting to the group pressures is used as the apperception that links the present with the past. Patterns of power arrangements, amount of participation, and interchanges of verbal and nonverbal behavior are interrelated with the actual content produced within the group setting. The therapist utilizes humor and optimism as well as seriousness and concern.

The initial stages of group therapy are for the promotion of sufficient gratification and positive interactions that will help to prevent early drop-outs. Only after the group shows some cohesion and loyalty does the therapist identify more critical inner conflicts and begin to move more actively into dealing with transference behavior.

The following sections are devoted to transference and countertransference issues frequently noted in adolescent groups. It is by no means a complete cataloging.

TRANSFERENCE PROBLEMS THAT OCCUR IN ADOLESCENT GROUPS

This discussion will be grouped into the following areas: attitudes toward authority and peers; acting out; silence; and somatization.

1. *Attitudes toward Authority and Peers.* One prevailing transference identified in the early sessions of adolescent groups is the active or passive rebellion against, and fear of accepting the leader, the clinic, agency, hospital, etc. The following is an excerpt of the ongoing dialogues among various members in a first session:

Member 1:   No one cares or really understands.

Member 2:   Yea, at school the teachers don't give a damn. They are interested only in their paychecks.

Member 3:   Oh, you should talk to my goody-good social worker. She spills the beans all over the place.

Therapist: And here?

(everyone laughs)

Member 1:   Well, you shrinks know it all.

Member 4:   Yes, but the difference is here you have a chance to get the opinion of kids your own age, but I don't like the one-way screen.

Member 1:   But I do like the fact that this is a group for us, exclusively, and our parents can't butt in.

This conversation continued about "butting in" parents, and the therapist commented: "You probably have some good reasons to distrust lots of people but things can't be perfect here either."

The handling of the early experiences of transferential feelings in the above instance was by way of allying with the adolescent, not assuming the role of the perfect authoritarian parental model that they have grown accustomed to expect. The rules described previously provide the adolescents with the knowledge that the discussions are highly confidential. They are permitted to state their angry feelings toward authority models in general and the therapist draws the discussion to the interacting group. As can be seen above, the associations went quickly to the group feelings about key figures in the past. The transference issue is played down and confrontation, rather than interpretation, is used in the early stages.

Allowing the adolescents to see how their peers and therapist pick-up their distorted projections in the present, rather than playing the role of nagging parent, fosters faster acceptance. A point of technique worthy to stress at this point is that the therapist, although he is an early ally of the adolescent's resistance (i.e. "you probably have some good reasons to distrust people"), he does not go to the extreme and attack the parent. No matter how bad the parent, only the child is allowed the privilege of condemnation, or otherwise the adolescent will retaliate against even the best meaning therapist and usually break treatment. Similarly, it is easier for the adolescents to attack the therapist than each other. This is desirable, for the therapist, in his response, shows a way of accepting criticism and anger without becoming irrational and over-emotional, a response that the adolescent may never have seen in the past. Gradually, when there is sufficient group cohesion and loyalty,

peers begin to interact more openly and deal with unjusti-
fied attacks of sarcasm, rivalry, belittling, jealousy, or guilt.
The following example is illustrative of multiple peer and
therapist transferences, which help to pave the way for
further therapy.

An eighteen-year-old, clever, overtalkative, grandiose
boy, John, who had earlier learned to cope with his marked
paranoid feelings in the group and who had trouble in coping with his anger toward his parents, reproached Elaine
sitting opposite him:

"How come you always look at her (therapist) and only
talk to her. Even now you don't want to look at me." Elaine
became flushed, awkward, and answered: "Shut up." The
group then discussed who looked at other people's eyes,
whether they remembered the color of their own eyes, etc.
Surprisingly, several members said they often forgot the
color of their own eyes. At this point the initial speaker
laughed and said:

John:	I remember a horse once who had one blue and one brown eye.
Elaine:	Just like my father.
Therapist:	Pardon?
Elaine:	Yea, like I say, I never look at people's eyes and I never realized until about three years ago that my father had one blue and one brown eye.
Various group members:	You mean you never looked at your father really to notice?
Therapist:	It's interesting that Elaine often looks at me, though, and no others.
John:	She's safer with you, you don't get angry at her.

Only the upper crust of the transference problem had been dealt with, namely Elaine's dependency upon and search for protective authority figures (i.e. therapist), and secondly, the peers' jealousy of a fellow group member. The underlying fear remains, the threat that if the patients allow themselves to develop close, tender bonds, they run the risk of being rejected, as in the past.

BODY LANGUAGE

Libidinal transference behavior is often observed through seductive flirtations, shyness, complimenting, applauding, and one's body geography. By the latter is meant the body postures, leanings, subtle touching, active pushing, or placing of one's feet in close proximity to the territorial space of an adjacent or oppositely seated member. Not to be overlooked is the marked use of cigarette passing, smoking, etc. Frequently, tension is broken by any, or a combination of, the above communications.

An example in the fifth month of this group demonstrates a libidinal transference. Over several months, John, who was the only black boy in the group, tried to befriend June, a very pretty, coquettish, blond girl, who consistently rejected him for being a show-off and a braggard. In one session after another, June rebuffed him. Finally, John reacted strongly and in a loud voice.

John: Yes, you are the stereotype of the Protestant, English, upper class, snob.

June: You are very wrong. I am Catholic, French Canadian, and middle class.

Therapist: And you are white.

The group fell silent, for the issue of color had, up to this point, not been discussed, although two members had brought in books dealing with the themes of prejudice and racial integration.

John broke the silence: "I guess when I make up my mind that people fall into certain slots, it is hard for me to change. Well, I guess I have that problem of wanting to know white girls, like June, because as you know, my mother is white."

The members looked from one to the other and almost simultaneously said that John had never told them this fact. The group turned to the therapist for confirmation and she had to agree that this session was the first time John had spoken of his parents' intermarriage.

Up until that point in treatment, the therapist had been aware only of John's distorted projective identification with June. This confrontation led the patient to disclose his close conflictual tie with his mother and his repetitious search for love and acceptance by white girls who always rejected him, such as June.

2. *Acting Out.* Acting out is interrelated to transference attitudes toward authority and peers, but the term is reserved for that type of uncontrolled, impulsive, manipulative behavior that shows little overt guilt or concern for the feelings of others. Hostile and sexual components are usually intertwined! The term is also applied to those emotional disorders of rebellion against society or frequent incidents of delinquent and criminal behavior. The outside is attacked rather than keeping the impulse internal, resulting in a display of anxiety patterns of action.

Our present culture has emphasized the right to attack and disagree rather than to suffer in silence. Today's adolescents come geared to fight the "establishment" and do not openly show the propensity for guilt, as do their own parents. This is not to say that guilt is not an essential underlying component.

The anger, revenge, and self-punitiveness that propel the acting out have a multitude of origins, such as fear and distrust of the therapist and treatment, fear of self-disclosure, projections of their own hostility and guilt feelings, and a defiance against being helped, predicated on a fear of future abandonment. The behavior of Laura, a fifteen-year-old who "acted out" outside the group by becoming illegitimately pregnant, will serve as an example of how such impulsive and masochistic behavior is brought into the group. This youngster was a somewhat obese, plain looking girl of dull-normal intelligence, whose mother died when she was ten, father died when she was fourteen, and foster father died when she was fifteen. Presently, she was being rejected by her aunt and uncle as unmanageable. She usually shouted in a defiant, childish way at everybody, but always sat close to the therapist. She frequently slapped her hand across her forehead, or on the table. Often, she lit matches and allowed them to burn down very close to her fingers. On one occasion the group room, which also served as a play room, was not cleared and Laura soon found three darts and held them in her hand in a taunting way. Jean, a clever peer leader, motioned to the dart board that was hanging directly behind the therapist's head. Members yelled "no" and "yes" and Laura aimed and threw the dart, which whistled by the therapist's ear. I kept very still and held out my open hand to Laura, saying nothing. The group pressures mounted. Laura looked to Jean for support, but she did not receive it, for she, too, had capitulated to the group's demands to desist. The girl put the darts in my hand. There was a sigh of relief from all, a silence and then a discussion of Laura's behavior. They told her: "You can't keep doing whatever you want. You have to learn some control! You are always hitting people!" Therapist: "Even yourself!" Laura: "I got so angry, I could explode! The

only time anyone pays attention to me is when I am bad."
Therapist: "And maybe it is easier for you to be bad than
sad." Laura's eyes filled with tears and she cried "nobody
wants me. The only friends I have in the world are here!"
The group members quickly banded together, offered sympathy and said they understood.

The therapist then said: "I wonder if putting all the
blame on Laura is right?" Jean: "Well, she threw them!"
Therapist: "I wonder if Laura would have thrown them
without some encouragement?" Quickly, with this cue, the
group members, usually fearful of attacking Jean, spoke up
and identified her as the culprit behind the scene. The therapist interpreted that Laura was the convenient one to act
out everyone's angry wishes. The whole group admitted they
were all excited, surprised that she had thrown the darts,
and felt such action should not be allowed. They also com-
plimented the therapist for being "real cool." This clinical
example demonstrates not only this girl's pathology, but how
the group used a scapegoat to ventilate a common group
impulse and how they banded together to regain control.

This same Laura, who became illegitimately pregnant
before entering the group, provided one of those crises in
which the therapist was called early on a Saturday morning.
She thought she was pregnant again! The conversation
lasted not more than five minutes. I instructed (not advised)
her to contact her social worker immediately and to go
with her to the hospital for consultation. In the following
meeting, she told the group of her close call and the aid the
therapist had provided. They agreed that this type of outside contact was justified and if they were in similar danger,
they might do the same. In this session, again goaded on by
many members, Laura pulled the microphone plug out of
the wall socket. The group took over and she was "com-
pelled" to put the plug back in, although she said defiantly:

"No I won't put *it* back in." Bill quickly spoke up: "Because you may get pregnant again if you put it back in!" Laura blushed and the group laughed raucously. Only much later did it become clear within the group that this girl's sexual acting out was a desperate plea for friendship and mothering.

It is not always possible for the therapist to remain cool and collected. The danger from the countertransference point of view is that sometimes the therapist's own childish unconscious wishes may contribute to the acting out. Letting a group go to the limit is not a form of neutral permissiveness, but often silent participation. At times, fear reactions are realistic and justified, but undue fear and panic on the part of the leader are quickly transmitted to the group. The leader's style certainly defines the degree of acting out that will be allowed. This issue will be returned to in the discussion of countertransference.

3. *Silence.* Silence, per se, is very difficult for adolescents to tolerate, especially in the early stages of treatment. Tension builds up quickly and regressive acting out follows. The use of silence as a group resistance occurs when there is marked fear of self-disclosure and as a technique of testing the therapist. Using the silent treatment with parents is probably one of the most effective ways of winning out in the interaction. The adolescent does not give in and produce words and feelings, but remains aloof and mysterious, as he has been taught by his parents and authority models who are overthreatened by closeness. The magic of silence in a group is that it heightens emotion and binds the group in a dilemma to find a way out of an impasse. Silence covers a wide spectrum, differing from one culture to another, and ranging from normal meditation to a schizoid isolated retreat. Depending upon one's experience, silence has come to be identified as tolerable and desirable, or feared and resented. The philosophy of "children are meant to be seen

but not heard" differs from the one that states that the child's wishes must be obeyed at all costs and every whimper accepted. Within the group, those members who overuse the mechanism of silence begin to play important roles, such as the positive head-nodder, the sad-brooder, and the defiant-starer. Not infrequently, the covert leader of the opposition in the group is a silent member who makes a nonverbal sign, such as an arched eyebrow or a threatening glare, a tap or raised finger, when his power is being thwarted. The stubborn pursed lips of the adolescent is often remarkably similar to the clenched teeth of the baby refusing to eat! It is because of the non-talking aspect of these members, that their subtlest behavior gives cues to the experienced observer. The tongue sucking and clacking, as well as the smirk that plays a tune of modulating rhythms across the lips, the flaring and dilating nostrils, the narrowing eyes, and the hunched shoulders are all part of the signals that are picked up by the alert and observant therapist.

To a monotonous tapping, I once asked: "What is so important to tell us?" Caught off guard, the patient broke the silence. Talkative peers and therapists often fall into the trap of doing the talking for the silent member long after such active help is needed. In this case, the silent one is continually assured that he is in no way responsible for the decisions being made. At times, one can easily relate present silent behavior to past transference models, while other cases seem unfathomable. I am not sure that simply finding out the causes of silence results in change, unless new patterns of interaction are concurrently developed. What is important however, is that the therapist become aware of the marked anxiety usually covered by this mechanism. To become "mute" is to lose the use of language, which distinguishes human interaction.

In a recent group, a handsome, well-dressed fifteen-year-old always sat to the extreme left of the one-way screen, in the corner of the room. He talked a little in the earlier sessions, and then withdrew, although it was clear he was following all the conversations. On a certain day, as the topic of drugs came up, Bill was very attentive, and I noted his heavy flushing and perspiring. As usual, the group carried on the discussion, used to his non-participation. At one point, certain members were praising the marvelous sensations of taking drugs, while others were trying to explain that they were dangerous, even from their own experiences. I was acting as a "neutral" referee, but on their questioning of where I stood on this issue, I replied: "If the drugs are so great and wonderful, I can understand why you won't give them up, because danger or no danger, there is probably nothing else so exciting and great." There was a reaction of perplexity and a sudden gush from Bill: "You weren't supposed to say something like that. It's your duty to warn them of the medical dangers." Immediately, inquiries came from the entire group and they focused on Bill. "What do you mean? How come you know so much?" Unable to hold his peers at bay, he replied: "O.K., I am a nark (narcotics) agent in my school. I think it is my duty to inform on the pushers . . ." His alliance with the police and his detective role in this group were immediately suspect, but Bill quickly vowed that he was not in the role of informer in this group. Part of the boy's silent attitude could be linked to not wanting to reveal his secret, but it gradually became clearer that he had identified a way of gaining self-esteem and importance to compete with his father, a retired army captain. He had an underlying fear of inadequacy and identified with the aggressor in this area. At home, he was also silent, because to speak was to incur the wrath of his father.

A silent, obese girl sat with her coat folded over her

lap during each session. One day she put the coat on the couch and I immediately asked: "So, are you ready to stop hiding and open up?" Susan: "Yes, I think it's about time. I thought when I came here I would be the craziest one, but I really see all of them have problems and are courageous enough to talk about them. For the last two years I really have been talking only to my animals. I collect all the strays. I walk in the middle of the night when there are no people about. I feel at home in the silence of the cemetery. When I see a crying kitten or hungry dog I take it home. But then when my mother wouldn't keep me any more, I lost them all. I was sent to a school for delinquent girls." Susan could be analyzed from many points of view. She feared that she would be seen as pathological, and, therefore, punished and ostracized. She felt helpless and was in a state of lonely grief, giving to the animals the love she so dearly wanted herself. This girl, after two years of treatment, made an excellent recovery, finished high school with top marks, lost 30 pounds, swam and exposed her body for the first time, and helped make remarkable changes in her detention home. One day, on a visit from the press to the detention home, she volunteered to discuss the need for a group therapy treatment program for all the girls. Today, she is an attractive, highly skilled nurse.

I recall a case of a silent, emotionless girl who literally never spoke, but never missed a session. She, however, doodled and always drew a clock and said hello and good-bye. She was a most peripheral member. On one occasion the subject of mysteries and ghosts was being discussed and she seemed somewhat interested. I said something to the effect of "if houses could only talk"—and turning to Alice "or if the face of your clock could talk, which has recorded all our sessions from the beginning to the end." Alice smiled and said: "I'm not very smart and I don't understand many things that are talked about here, but I like it. When I draw my clock's face I mark the time we start and the time we finish. I know for this amount of time where I really have been and it is important to me." In some real ways, this young woman's regularity of coming and her acceptance for the first time in a group, helped establish her identity, i.e. her existence in time.

There are numerous transferential reasons for silence, ranging from the sulky child to defiance, anger, and fear of loss of control. Usually, not more than one excessively silent member can be tolerated in a group. Non-threatening silent members blend in much more easily than those members showing ambivalence and anger, but wielding a great deal of power by their strong passive-aggressive tactics. When the "group as a whole" shows silence, the need is to discover what pattern of resistance and transference is present at that particular time.

4. *Somatization.* Actual somatizations occurring in the group, or reports of them, serve to identify how the individual has learned to cope with stress over an extended period of time. Symptoms range from headaches, flushing, and palpitations, to fainting, seizure-like behavior, encopresis, vomiting, and hypochondriasis. Symptoms present a physical reality that is "better" than the elusive problems: "I'm really sick, not cuckoo." Adolescents hold onto somatic symptoms instead of coming to grips with emotional problems, and they do so in both individual and group forms of treatment. In my experience, their use of somatic complaints does not occupy the proportion of time as it does in the adult patient population. To be healthy and alive are much more positive concerns of the young!

At times, it is possible to link physical symptomatology with specific transferential objects, and, in other cases, one clarifies the ways all the members somatize in stress and how peers, parents, and siblings respond to this behavior. The following excerpts will serve as brief examples:

Ann, a pretty, shy, passive-aggressive girl, kept staring at her finger nails, and a boy next to her began to look at them and said: "You bite them?" Ann: "Yes, but it's not a problem, I like them." Sandra: "You suck them?" Ann: "No, I eat my nails." Therapist: "You don't chew them down very far?" Ann: "No, I don't like to hurt myself." Sandra: "Have you ever tried to stop?" Ann: "I can't." Almost all members then gave suggestions for solving the problem: e.g., use nail polish, dip the fingers in something foul tasting, wear gloves, etc. John laughed and said: "Why not find out why you do it." Therapist: "Probably many members of the group have different ways of handling stress." All members chimed in with their respective somatizations: nausea, stomach ache, and tightness in the chest.

Rhonda said: "I had nothing to do with my seizure. They found me unconscious—well, I could hear them a little. They rushed me to the hospital. That was one of the few times in my life I saw my father upset. Ordinarily he never talks but when I'm sick he gets very upset because he had an aneurysm eight years ago and he is always afraid he is going to die."

The group became very concerned and worried about Rhonda. The therapist remarked: "But you don't seem to be very upset." John added: "Yes, she is enjoying it and she really is quite gay." From the group therapy point of view the aim for the time being is to reduce the tension and anger emanating from her cravings for love and her own fears of dying.

Sudden experiences of headache, weakness, and desires to go to the toilet usually reveal anger, sadness, revenge, or regressive trends. As a final example, I will mention the case of an asthmatic attack a young woman experienced at a point when the group was talking about angry feelings toward fathers. She was discussing her memory of when her daddy rocked her and that he always smoked a pipe. "I hated the smoke, I could hardly breathe." At that moment in the group session, an asthma attack began. Fear ensued but the therapist cautioned for calm and opened the window "to give more air." The attack abated shortly and, in great distress, the girl, crying, told us that it was her first such attack in a year. I had identified how the girl was being choked by the recall of the smoke. Opening the window and finding air seemed like the only course of action! Doubtless, other possibilities existed, but the "giving" aspect of the therapist in the here-and-now probably induced a positive realistic approach to a crisis in which words were superfluous. Later, this patient talked of "air" as the "breath of life."

A common feature of all the transference issues discussed is the defensive nature of continuing to reuse patterns of behavior that prevent self-disclosure of the thoughts and feelings that the patients feel will result in catastrophe. The patients discover that they are not ostracized or rejected for their "bad" or "sinful" thoughts and behavior and, in fact, instead of disastrous consequences, they experience relief of symptom, gratification, and acceptance. Lateral transference to peers, as well as to the therapist, occurs. A domineering member may be responded to as an authority or parental figure. Like transference of thoughts and feelings to the therapist, the uncovering of transference to a peer in the group is relatively unimportant unless blended with emotional significance.

COUNTERTRANSFERENCE IN GROUPS IS STRONGER THAN
IN INDIVIDUAL SESSIONS

Countertransference, feelings and reactions stimulated

in the group therapist, is stronger in groups than in individual practice, and especially so in the pressured atmosphere created by adolescents. Adolescents invade the therapist's "privacy" to a much greater degree, by using personal inquiries, needling, sarcasm, put-downs, and direct attacks. They do this in a more open and defiant manner than adults, who are more respectful of the therapist's role, and more willing to accept patiently his formulations. Therapists who are novices in adolescent groups often complain of being insulted and treated with no respect, i.e. "they don't want to settle down or be serious." When they expect the adolescent to behave like an adult, they overlook the "playing around" behavior that can provide a real fiber of communication for analysis. In the earnest desire to get down to business, many therapists "unwittingly" block the adolescent group by their own rejecting attitudes.

The dilemma clearly posed for the therapist working with adolescents is how to maintain an intermediate position on the chronological and maturational ladders; he will never be accepted as a peer, and he should not retreat into an autocratic judgmental role.

Therapists who have low frustration tolerance for anger, acting out, anxiety, fear, or repressive behavior, make poor candidates for work with adolescents. The wish to not be reminded of their own childhood and adolescent rebellions (overt and covert), and their overstress on conformity tend to suppress the adolescent group. Some therapists do not want to be exposed to sick or naughty behavior while, on the other hand, some might "over-need" this kind of stimulation. Usually, perfectionistic therapists rule themselves out as leaders with adolescents. A danger, however, lies in the leader who likes to rap and identify with the adolescent to the unrealistic level of being a peer. When the therapist goes this far, he loses his distinguishing attributes as a therapist.

COUNTERTRANSFERENCE REACTIONS THAT IMPAIR AND BLOCK THERAPY

Countertransference, in the broadest framework, covers all of the therapist's reactions in the group setting. This chapter is limited only to those repetitive countertransference behaviors that, if unacknowledged and unmodified, impair and block therapy. Successful working through of undesirable countertransference reactions produces new awareness and opens up a new fund of information, as well as freeing more effective ways of solving problems. Intensive, long-term supervision provides some of these safeguards for the junior therapist—while, hopefully, for the senior one, discussion with peers and working behind a one-way screen will provide on-going learning and growth experience.

With these general comments, the following inter-related areas will be briefly highlighted: omnipotence, privacy versus self-disclosure, "overidentification" with the adolescent, blind spots, and somatizations.

OMNIPOTENCE IN THERAPISTS

Omnipotent therapists encourage "overdependency" in group members and prevent autonomous growth. The need for the therapist to be powerful, all-knowing, and highly successful prevents the adolescent from open competition. The threat that the adolescent felt from omnipotent adults in the past, he now feels from the therapist. The image of infallibility cannot be matched by the adolescent and the leader remains an aloof untouchable. His professional scholarliness blocks participation, i.e. "You always know everything, even before I say it." The patient learns that if he challenges the leader's omnipotent stance, the leader's narcissism is hurt. Omnipotent therapists usually strive to have the best and fastest cures and are acutely disappointed if this does not occur. When the omnipotent type of counter-transference is dealt with in supervision, the young therapist may feel hurt and criticized.

ADOLESCENTS WANT OMNIPOTENT THERAPISTS

It is very important to realize that in the early stages, omnipotent attitudes are encouraged by the adolescents themselves. The fantasy is realized early in therapy of an all-powerful protector, who will solve all their problems. It is only after this initial period that the clash of transference and countertransference becomes open, and if not resolved, it usually leads to a crisis or fragmentation of the group. The exhibitionistic leader is a strong contrast to the silent, distant one, but each may show equally strong power driven tendencies. Exhibitionistic leaders are very much in vogue today. However, the seductive, charismatic aspects of exhibitionism are well known and after an initial period of hero worship, this type of therapist is often unable to deal with the threatening, emerging challenges of group members.

FEAR OF SELF-DISCLOSURE

Closely interwoven with the above discussion is the therapist's fear of self-disclosure. One extreme defense is to withdraw to the group's periphery in order to maintain safeguards against disclosure of problems that have caused hiding or flight in the past. Although the surface manner would indicate maturity and self-control, it soon becomes clear that such therapists are rigid and it is difficult for them to show flexibility, warmth, or spontaneity in group interaction.

The therapist whose countertransference propels him to share too many of his feelings and problems with the group is disclosing himself too much. His need for too much closeness and acceptance causes arousal of erotic feelings and sibling rivalry. The identity crisis of the adolescent is further aggravated by a therapist who burdens the group with his puzzling disclosures. Excessive closeness impairs the therapist, since he does not present a model to the adolescent.

THE MORE ACTIVE AND INVOLVED, THE MORE SELF-DISCLOSURE

As group therapists become more active and involved, their self-disclosures increase. The curiosity of the adolescent group cannot be easily curtailed. In the traditional model of psychotherapy, if the therapist is asked a personal question, he responds with statements such as "what do you think," or "what are your fantasies." Adolescents do not easily accept such therapy tactics; furthermore, they will learn to turn right around and throw the same questions back at the therapist. Many inquiries are natural and realistic and they deserve an honest answer, as the therapist would expect when he asks the members questions. Mutual respect for each other's privacy is easily gained if the therapist does not respond in a frightened suspicious manner when the adolescent begins to climb into his sacred chambers, but good-humoredly declares that they have tested him enough. The rights of the members to reach a point of self-revelation and then say: "That's enough, no more," also applies to the therapist. There are no hard and fast rules in this area.

Some therapists have good flexibility and can disclose areas about themselves in a natural and spontaneous manner. At the same time, they can set down safeguards for personal liberties in the group.

IDENTIFICATION WITH THE ADOLESCENT

The therapist can gain vicarious satisfaction by helping the group act out his countertransference wishes and expectations. At times, the therapist may actively encourage "getting it all out" and spearhead the attack. An opposite tactic comes from the over-neutral leader who "innocently" does not call a halt or set controls in time. Instead, he waits permissively to see how far things will go. His "shrugs" and "hmms" are interpreted as affirmative communications when they match the needs of the group. An example comes to mind of two young therapists who went once weekly to a home for delinquent boys. The "permissive strangers" encouraged an open discussion of the "problems" the boys were having in the home. Covertly, they allied with the adolescents against the regime and in the third session the group room was demolished. Perhaps the potential for attack was already in the delinquent population of the group, but it seemed to be triggered off by the awareness that the therapists did not like the institution either.

SEDUCTIVE THERAPISTS

There is a difference between the group therapist who is warm and friendly and the one who engages in seductiveness, flirtation, erotic interaction, and unnecessarily bringing the group discussion back to sexual themes. Sometimes, watching T.V. playbacks, one becomes aware of this kind of non-verbal message from the group therapist. For example, a young, handsome therapist rubbed his nose a total of five times in one session, each occurring prior to an interaction with a specific female patient. Each time, she continued her discussion of her ambivalent love feelings for her father.

In a recent group, a very quiet, serious, therapist could always be made to blush or squirm in his chair by the pretty girls. They soon told him that although he was very quiet, he knew how to use his "beautiful eyes."

SOMATIZATIONS AND BLIND SPOTS

The therapist may become aware of his countertransference through his own physiological responses prior to, during, and following a group session. Blushing, perspiring, feeling cold, hot, nauseous, crampy, chest pressure, dry mouth, or teeth clenching, to name a few, occur from time to time in us all in various degrees of stressful interactions. Falling asleep and yawning may sometimes be due to fatigue but it is not infrequently related to flight patterns due to emerging rage or other negative feelings that are unacceptable.

"Blind spots" are usually searched for when the therapist realizes he is at an impasse with the group. Being observed directly—from the one-way mirror or over a good quality closed circuit television—is the most efficient way of learning about the therapist's "blind spots," as well as other manifestations of countertransference. Often, supervisors who have no access to evaluating the live session, must listen to trainee reports or, preferably, audio-taped sessions, and unnecessarily miss out on many transference-countertransference events simply because they are not reported consciously by the supervisee. A supervisor can be surprised when he compares what the student says he is doing with what he actually does.

After a study of transference-countertransference patterns of communication, perhaps one feels that it should be possible to draw up a portrait of the "ideal" leader dealing with adolescent groups. Probably no such person really exists, but I would consider the following qualities extremely useful for a group therapist: adequate skills and experience, flexibility, spontaneity, enthusiasm, trust, honesty, optimism, a good sense of humor, an adequate frustration tolerance, and a dedicated responsibility to the care of the young.

Creative Activities

JOANN VICK, A.C.S.W. AND IRVIN A. KRAFT, M.D.

Many papers and books describe adolescence in our culture. Authors agree on such characteristics as turmoil, rebellion, identity seeking, upsurging sexuality, enhanced creativity, sudden depressive episodes, and expanded self-world awareness. Therapists hold various theoretical notions about the socio-psychodynamics of disturbed youth.

ADOLESCENT GROWTH PRODUCES BOTH REGRESSION AND INCREASED PERCEPTIVENESS

Our conceptualization of adolescence assumes a revival of the oedipal period in our adaptational framework of reference, a strong influence of cultural and subcultural forces, and that the ego of adolescents undergoes various vicissitudes, including strong regressive trends. In adolescence, there is a partial regression in feelings toward an object relationship. This explains the increased need for a love object and the need for union with this love object. The need is accompanied by the fear that the regression may go too far and result in a "giving up" or dissolution of the self. This fear explains much of the adolescent's defiant and rebellious behavior and his sudden, unpredictable changes of love object. Along with this partial regression, there is an increase in perceptiveness, directed both inwardly and toward the outside world. This increased perceptiveness explains the enthusiasm that is sublimated in many cases in artistic and intellectual endeavors. The partial regression in love object relationships is an ego phenomenon that seems to be necessary for the process of growth and maturation of the adolescent's identity.

DANCE, POETRY, AND OTHER ARTISTIC ACTIVITIES

This regressive phenomenon of adolescence is a basis for our attempt, in the group treatment of adolescent girls, to use a variety of artistic activities to expand the group therapeutic approach described in previous chapters. These included dance or rhythmic movement, music, poetry, graphic art, both active and passive, and a light-box. This light-box produces variegated never-repeated patterns of color on a plastic screen and promotes fascination, fixation of attention, and fantasy. Auxiliary therapists, who were specialists in their fields, were utilized, when indicated.

SETTING AND COMPOSITION OF AN
ADOLESCENT GROUP OF GIRLS

The group that is the subject of this chapter met for a period of eighteen months in a separate two-story building that is a part of a children's medical center with impressive new high-rise architecture. Twenty-seven girls, ranging in age from thirteen to seventeen, participated in the group. The average length of participation was fourteen meetings, with individuals varying from a single session to fifty-one sessions. They represented a wide variety of presenting problems including: anorexia nervosa, obesity, school drop-out and failure, drug abuse, sexual acting-out, premature marital plans, depression, rebellion, withdrawal, hysteria, suicidal attempts, and psychotic behavior.

Since a psychiatric consultation preceded entry into the hospital for almost all the girls, they were aware by virtue of their referral that the group was the major therapeutic approach. However, concommitantly, two of the girls were also referred to art therapy, several attended individual psychotherapy sessions, and six were seen at times of crisis either individually or in family therapy.

Influencing the group gestalt was the inclusion of a variety of mental health trainees. These included students at all levels, including post-doctoral, involved in such disciplines as pediatrics, medicine, psychiatry, psychology, and social work. Although these trainees and other specialists usually attended and fitted in with the group's processing of interactions, the core leadership of the group remained constant. One of the core leaders participated in each of the group experiments independent of the group meetings in order to better identify with the mood and feelings experienced by the group of girls.

The continued involvement of the group with the visiting, temporary co-leaders, offered the girls a variety of experiences they could later utilize in better understanding their interaction and behavior with other adults. When transferential responses and behavior became obvious with reference to the leaders or visitors, the group was urged to talk about them. The girls seemed to tolerate new additions rather well and adaptability to change became an unwritten axiom of their group.

AN OLDER, DRUG USER MEMBER LEADS FOR A WHILE

We considered at one point, owing to the ever-present involvement of teenagers in drug abuse, using as an adjunctive leader, an older adolescent girl, Mary, who had survived and "kicked" drugs, including heroin. We speculated that she could, by this role, consolidate her own gains and experiences, as well as guide others, but she proved unable to handle it adequately. After a few sessions, she begged to be excused from this responsibility and the group proceeded without any significant retardation in its movement.

The original group began with four members led by two staff social workers, Joann, the originator of the group, and Mary. The psychiatrist author was involved, since he had seen most of the girls in consultation and referred them to the group. Since he also treated a few individually, at times, in addition to their group experiences, his involvement with the group furnished an interesting contrast to the adults who regularly attended as assistant therapists and leaders.

OBSERVER-PARTICIPANTS

Regular observer-participants included a medical

student who had originally been on a first-year research elective with us and who then aligned himself with the group, attending its weekly sessions long after his elective terminated. He managed an appearance despite his regular student obligations and clinical functions, and his quiet, shy presentation of himself contrasted with the bouyancy and verve of many of the other adults involved with the group.

Our training program for para-therapists, in contradiction to the traditional triad of social work, clinical psychology, and psychiatry, uses housewives, pediatricians, sociologists, and child care workers. For a while the group also included one certified family practice physician, who began to work with Lynn, a 16-year-old borderline psychotic. This family physician followed Lynn individually in our unit and in home visits after her discharge. He was also a group participant-observer while Lynn worked in the group. The medley of therapists seemed to aid rather than disrupt Lynn's therapeutic progress. The group offered her a central source of friendship, peership, understanding, and familiarity which drew her from the brink of suicide on several occasions.

BACKGROUND OF THE MEMBERS

The girls shared similar sociocultural backgrounds, with the traditional middle-class standards of a southwestern metropolitan area. The basic familial orientation to religion was Protestant. The group was composed entirely of middle-class Caucasians since psychiatric consultation and treatment for adolescent, middle-class black girls was still infrequent in the patient populations seen by the authors. The families to whom the recommendation for this kind of therapy was made were accepting, and some parents saw the group as a way of protecting their daughters through the wilds of adolescence.

Most of the girls came from comfortable physical surroundings and had a wide variety of cultural experiences. All were of high or above average intelligence without any obvious handicaps of basic learning. All had some personal exposure to the drug subculture, usually speaking its vocabulary knowledgeably. Most had experimented with marijuana, and regular usage was not uncommon. Other drugs were known in some way to all of them and several complained of having experienced "bad trips." None used heroin.

Sexual experiences ranged widely among them. They often discussed coital activity in more bold terms than we had heard in similar groups ten years before. Open discussion of the merits of different birth-control methods vied with the expressed wishes for continuity with the steady boy friend, since sexual intercourse seemed the glue of "going steady."

DREAMS WERE VERBALIZED

Dreams frequently became the focus for most if not all of an entire session and they helped the girls in their pattern of tagging their groupmates with a psychodynamic nickname. Jane, for example, related a recurring dream in which she saw a series of people having difficulties getting up or down curbs. This was particularly so for a lady pushing a baby in a carriage. The group quickly arrived at the belief that the curbs represented obstacles in life and that Jane reflected in them her own anxiety about growing up and facing the problems of becoming independent. At times, when Jane reported on daily problems, the others reminded her that she was approaching a curb in her daily life.

As we sought safe, yet emotional, outlets for the group, we turned to poetry, psychodrama, and body movement techniques. For example, emotional understanding of the feelings around a situation emerged when Carol dramatized them by writing a poem which she later shared with the group.

Carol was in the 8th grade of a parochial school and the youngest of four siblings. Her parents divorced when she was six years of age and Carol lived with her mother. Her father was hospitalized twice and diagnosed as having a manic-depressive illness. Her mother never dated or remarried, exhibiting martyr traits in a passive-dependent personality. The onset of adolescence ushered in constant arguments with her mother. On one occasion Carol threatened her mother with a gun. An older sister, who had the role of watching while the mother worked, married and left home. Carol, not yet fourteen, secretly began to date an eighteen-year-old boy. Recently, her mother had begun to accuse Carol of drug usage and argued that Carol's mood swings were caused by drugs.

Carol, embarked on a journey of seeking her "freedom," did not know how to relate to authority. Her relationship with her mother accentuated this difficulty as well as the long exposure to the unstable personality traits of both parents.

Group therapy for Carol aimed at utilizing peer influence for self-exploration, helping her define her dependency versus independency conflicts, obtaining support for implementing positive goals, deemphasizing adult "superiority," focusing on her own resources for self-growth and dignifying and promoting her creative outlets. Her mother was referred to a family agency for casework psychotherapy. In addition to a good intellect, Carol brought to the group her talent in playing the guitar by ear, her poetry, and her ability to relate and verbalize her feelings.

In the group, Carol was very dramatic. Her creative writing reflected a dramatic despair and confusion over her own identity and life goals. She presented herself in the "costume" of a hippie and talked as if she were quite experienced in drug usage. She was frightened of her dependency needs since they were not met at home, and she tried to grow up too fast by belonging to an older group that took care of her. She became "the baby" of our group and was impressed by the older members and the limits placed upon her by them. Carol wanted definite limits but at the same time needed a place to "grow" and expand as she felt suppressed at home. She was not allowed to paint her own room at home, plant a garden, have friends in if they had long hair, etc.

Carol read her poem in her typical dramatic manner, but it produced feelings of empathy and closeness among all the members, encouraging the older girls to continue their involvement with Carol and with each other.

Why am I in this wretched interior?
What is this envelope that led me to
  this slum?

If only I could know or understand;
  this shamble reminds me of that
  morbid house where I survived with
  that butcher.

Oh the darkness, the aching in my
  mind, the blackness, am I insane?
I can remember happiness once, but
  what is becoming of me now?

But I mustn't think of the past
   I must concentrate on the present.
It all seems so familiar, yet I can't
   recall why.
I must open that door.

Why is there no light?
Where are those voices?
These hands, they are taking me
   somewhere.
But where? I can't see.
The echoing silence, that pain in
   my shoulder.
It's all so strange, like a nightmare.
This is agony I have never felt before.
I'm falling.

My head aches.
I can't tell where I am;
It seems like a staircase.
I see light now.
I am no more.

Like other group therapies, each exploration by the group of a member's difficulties enhanced the cohesiveness. Some of the girls tested their parents with subtle or obvious distortions, producing some heated reactions, such as: "All you do there is talk about drugs and sex! No wonder she gets worse that way! We won't let her go back next week!" In this way some of these girls gained the responses they chronically elicited from their parents but became lost members to the group and its benefits.

REAL LIFE PORTRAYED IN PSYCHODRAMA

These kinds of conflicts with parents were acted out in

various ways. One girl enacted how she was going to leave home to marry an "undesirable boy" and the group, in turn, assumed a maternal role in trying to stop her. Jane then acted out against the group as she had with her family. She "ran away" for a period and showed her deeply felt hostility by appropriate expressions to the group. For a while psychodrama and the reality of her life seemed to merge. The running away from home theme remained prominent in the group's thinking and reactions for several sessions.

DISCOVERY THROUGH DANCE

Discovery therapy, a form of dance therapy, was developed in our day hospital program. It utilizes pantomime, directed nonverbal fantasy activities, body awareness through motion, and other devices which aid movement communication. When new members entered the group, the old members formed a circle and held hands. The new member had to break her way in, emphasizing the difficulties of such an entry situation—and at the same time creating empathy in the older members for the new ones.

During their first *dance therapy* movement session, the girls began the action with tenseness, giggles and self-consciousness. They were invited to throw a ball to each other rhythmically, engage in body stretches alone and with partners, and then comment on the movements that were made. More complicated balancing movements, involving the support of another's body weight, came later; these involved standing up and sitting down together, face-to-face and back-to-back. As their trust increased, the girls eagerly spoke for turns at being caught by two other girls as they let their bodies fall stiffly off balance forward, backward, and sideways. Concentrated involvement emerged when "tuning in" occurred with mirror movements to a partner's slow, spontaneous body action; there was a relaxed quality to their body movement, and warmth and support began to enter their relationships.

Throughout the life of the group, we found that psychodrama and movement therapy formed natural outlets for the girls. They seemed to enjoy exaggerating their plight and acting out their desires. Poetry written by the group members proved more stimulating and profitable than published poetry. Music allowed their moods to grow, and it provided a background in which communication flowed more freely. Each girl brought her own favorite records and discussed the music with the group. The music was often turned down so that they could talk better and the group could not hide behind the music by just sitting and listening.

Pictures from magazines depicting people who were displaying emotions of different kinds were passed out to the girls and they composed stories about them, but after a while we found this to be a useless technique since they could not relate the pictures to themselves. Another unpopular activity was using the light-box and looking at its mood-creating colors and shapes, because this process encouraged introspection and deemphasized the group. Finally, in response to this activity, one girl said: "Look, I came here to be with people and not to be alone again!"

Members' dependency on the group shone forth in their determination to get to the meetings: one girl required a note to get out of school earlier each time; hitch-hiking and bus riding were tried; although considered by most of the patients as risky for promptness. The girls regarded the group as a sort of status symbol and they greeted each other at school and other gathering places with such comments as, "See you on Thursday." However, not every girl exposed to the group liked it, maintained attendance, or regarded the group in an elite manner.

Psychodrama, the creating of poetry, and dance therapy proved valuable aids to the more traditional methods of adolescent group therapy techniques in loosening inhibitions, creating patterns of closeness, and stimulating communication.

Art Therapy

KATHLEEN GIDEON, A.T.R. AND NORMAN S. BRANDES, M.D.*

Art therapy provides a medium of expression particularly suited to the needs and problems of young patients. Encouraged to experiment with the art media in a free and uninhibited manner aimed at the development of creative expression, the adolescent patients can identify previously unidentifiable emotions. It further provides a method of expressing their thoughts and feelings to each other in the group as well as in their interpersonal relationships outside the group. Discussion by the group members gives them the

*The authors of this chapter wish to acknowledge the valuable help of Miss Virginia Tindall, O.T.R., in composing the original plan for this chapter.

opportunity of validating their ideas and feelings within the limits of the reality established by the art therapist and other group members.

NATURE OF THE ART THERAPY GROUP

The adolescent art therapy group is a "loose" group. For the most part, the patients are chosen in terms of chronological age, rather than diagnosis. Despite the diagnostic differences most of the adolescent patients are seen as coping with similar problems such as biologically determined sexual feelings, identity conflicts, need for emancipation, and fearfulness over the responsibilities and ensuing demands of adulthood. At one time or another, these universal problems of adolescence appear in their art work, often disguised by other emotional pathology. Each adolescent patient is encouraged to be aware and respectful of his peers' uniqueness. Expressiveness, not artistic technique, is encouraged. Stimulated by the drawings and paintings, the group discussions are guided by the art therapist toward the goal of assisting each adolescent to become aware of his uniqueness as a person within the accepting atmosphere of the group. Many areas are opened up that are brought back to their individual psychotherapy and traditional group psychotherapy sessions by these young patients for further exploration.

THE ART THERAPY ROOM

The art therapy room is designed to encourage spontaneity as well as a feeling of freedom to discuss intimate things. Half of the room contains comfortable chairs placed semi-circularly and the other part of the room is reserved for the art equipment and work area. Some of the basic art equipment consists of the following: (1) A large, flat, high, soft-textured (to hold tacks easily) painting wall that the patient works on in a standing position. (2) A long table built like a buffet, that serves as a common pallet; it holds: (a) large cups of water-based tempera in a wide variety of colors; (b) large brushes, one, two and three inches wide; (c) large pieces of colored chalk and charcoals; (d) a stack of 24 by 18-inch white paper that can be placed anywhere on the painting wall; (e) a 24 by 40-inch paper, sometimes brown, that serves as the "group painting;" and (f) an ample supply of thumb tacks, extra water, and cleaning towels and erasers.

RULES ARE SIMPLE

New patients are acquainted with the simple art equipment, told that expression not skill is important, and asked to produce as many paintings or drawings as they like (the average seems to be two per patient). Also, they are told about the simple rules: (1) They must not throw paint at anyone else in the group; and (2) they must not destroy or deface another patient's work.

Sometimes, it becomes necessary to introduce other rules as a reaction to what is going on in the group. One day, a sixteen-year-old painted his hand with gold paint and pressed his hand to a sheet of paper. He became fascinated with this prospect and soon painted his entire two legs and arms. The idea spread to some of the other young group members and, in a few minutes, developed into a playful but distracting resistance to any kind of serious therapy. After some discussion about this behavior, it was decided to make a new rule: "No body painting."

THREE YOUNG PEOPLE WHO RESPONDED TO ART THERAPY

In an active inpatient–outpatient psychiatric service, patients may be referred to art therapy for brief periods and then, for various reasons, fade out of psychotherapy altogether. However, because they are determined to do something about the way they deal with problems, certain young patients "stick it out" for a significantly longer time. Three of them stand out in our recent memories who illustrate some advantages in the exposure of emotional disturbances to the creative expression of artistic production.

ANGRY, COMBATIVE DOUG

Doug, a sixteen-year-old high school student, was admitted to our university psychiatric hospital because of social isolation, temper tantrums, and angry outbursts that appeared to be uncontrollable.

His problems became evident three years prior to admission when teasing and aggressive behavior with his friends resulted in frequent fights. His siblings and peers became increasingly frightened of his explosive behavior and avoided him, causing further isolation and withdrawal. Doug claimed that most of his frequent clashes were a result of various groups singling him out as the person to fight when they wanted to test the courage and bravery of one of their members.

In the early part of his five-month hospital stay, Doug had managed to duplicate his pre-hospital school situation of almost total alienation from his peers. During art therapy sessions, his energies and attention were focused mostly on his art productions rather than verbal interaction with others in the group. This device allowed Doug to stay close to the art therapy group members without having to provoke them to the usual angry, retaliatory combat.

His first productions were esthetically pleasing and evoked some admiration from his peers[1]. He seemed pleased with this recognition of his talents. He attended the group voluntarily and regularly but remained silent during the conversations that followed the art work.

His drawings began to evidence some of his fantasies of being a powerful super human figure[2, 3]. He still withheld comment about his drawings and showed little response to the comments of others in the group. As his group became a more comfortable place for Doug, he began to risk some of his feelings in a more concrete form. After drawing the picture of the runner[4], he spontaneously put in the words "prison" and "home" on direction signs, commenting to the group that he felt like the hospital was a prison for him.

Art therapist: How does the rest of the group feel about the runner running away from prison and to home?

Ann: Well . . . this place is like a prison sometimes.

Jim: I hate those screens on the windows.

Mike: Yeah . . . its like you're sentenced here or something.

Finding that others in the group shared similar feelings seemed to free Doug to continue verbally. He began commenting on some of the pictures done by the other group members.

In later sessions, he started to express, in poster art form, some of his ideas and began to reveal his past history and present situation with the other group patients[5, 6]. At about this time, Doug began to talk in the after-painting session and share his reactions to the paintings and interpretations of the others in the group.

With the encouragement of some of the group members, he began experimenting with abstract painting[7]. For Doug's

CASE 1.   DOUG

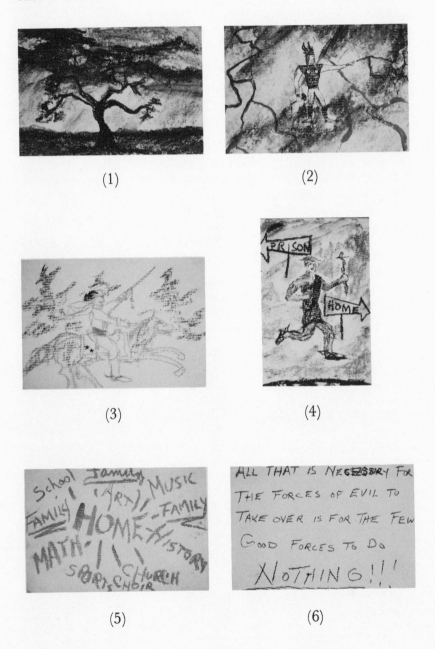

(1)

(2)

(3)

(4)

(5)

(6)

(7)

needs and conflicts, art therapy provided a less threatening environment than the rest of the hospital and it gave him vital time to learn to become part of a group.

PATTY—NAZISM AND ALIENATION

Patty was a seventeen-year-old, who was admitted because of extreme withdrawal, explosive outbursts, conspicuous immaturity, and fierce obsessions with Nazism.

Her history in school was not remarkable until age fifteen, when she began to exhibit explosive behavior when things did not go well. Her academic performance began to fall rapidly and her social behavior regressed. At this time, she had become obsessed with thoughts of Nazism.

Patty, the oldest of six siblings, was raised in a discordant atmosphere where finances and religion presented major problems. Her father, a minister for eighteen years, became a history instructor and continued to preach at a small church. His wife, unable to accept any kind of "domination," could not accept his ideas and feelings about religion. In rebellious fashion, she joined a more liberal church, protesting not only the religion of Patty's father but also the financial bind in which he placed the family by not being a successful minister in his own church.

Initially, Patty seemed eager to illustrate her situation and share it with other group members. She explained to the group that she felt she was being pulled by the opposite influences of her doctor and her mother[1]! The group showed interest and concern, and wondered why her mother was represented by the dark side of the drawing. Patty did not explain this darkness to the group. However, in subsequent art therapy sessions, she continued to illustrate problems. She expressed her struggle with her loneliness and her battle against being overly dependent on her therapist, which brought about interest and support from the group[2].

After a while, Patty showed signs of an uneasy toleration of the closeness and support of her peers in the group and she began to paint scenes and other expressions of blood and violence[3, 4]. The group's interest in this type of subject was short-lived and Patty was soon pushed aside from the group discussions.

After several weeks of these alienating paintings, Patty again began to express some of her real life problems: her home situation [5], which was disintegrating during her hospital stay; and her anxiety over her dependence on her doctor. She chose to illustrate this conflict of dependency on her doctor by painting a dependency relationship between mother and child[6].

To illustrate her feelings of loneliness and sadness, she represented herself as a flower set in a dark blue background[7].

Art therapist: Patty, tell us about that painting—what does it mean?

Another patient: Whatever it is, it looks blue and sad. Is it supposed to be a flower?

Psychiatric resident: Patty, if that is a flower, it looks like it is bursting.

CASE 2. PATTY

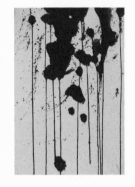

(1)   (2)

(3)   (4)

(5)   (6)

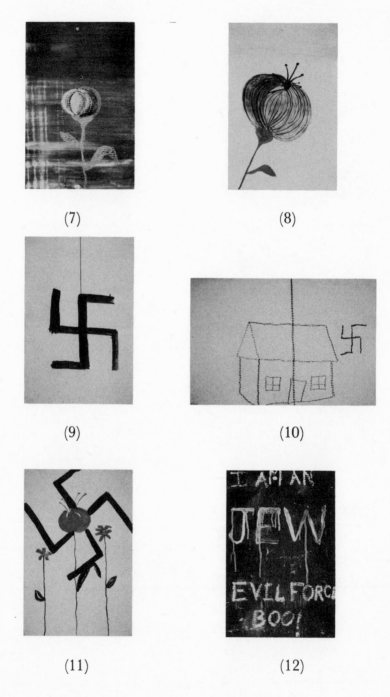

(7)

(8)

(9)

(10)

(11)

(12)

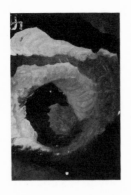

(13)

(14)

(15)

(16)

(17)

(18)

Patty: I used blue because I feel blue. I feel lousy . . . alone . . . like that flower. Several sessions later she repeated the flower theme, saying that things were looking brighter[8].

Her swastika paintings illicited anger and rejection from the group[9]. The reaction seemed to stimulate Patty and for many of the following sessions, she continued to paint and draw the same subject with further avoidance reactions from the group.

As this swastika theme continued, it became more evident that it seemed to reflect her still unidentified feelings about her seething conflicts of alienation from her family[10]. The picture of the bulging bud which appeared in previous paintings on the swastika[11] produced curious reactions from the group. They questioned her use of this unusual flower, "Is that yourself, this flower, inside the swastika?" The group members wondered if she felt like a Jew who was alienated and isolated in a Nazi world. She dealt with this interpretation in a subsequent art therapy session[12].

Then her need to bring about rejection with the swastika seemed to diminish, although she retained it as her signature. She concentrated more on keeping with the activities and interest of the group. As she became more accepted by her peers, she became more influenced by their activity and painted abstract paintings[13, 14].

She started to share with the group her concerns about a boy friend[15]. With this new kind of closeness and trust that developed in the group, she was able to talk about her bewildering sexual feelings[16, 17].

Patty was forced to leave the group in order to start working in her first job[18]. This was felt to be a realistic step toward the kind of independence from her family ties that she was planning.

Greg was in the same adolescent age bracket with Patty and Doug. During his early years, Greg had been seen by numerous pediatricians all over the country to evaluate his extreme activity and peculiar periods of non-response to people. He was thought to be a restless, hyperactive child with possible brain damage. As he grew, his psychological difficulties became more apparent.

All of the hospital personnel who worked with Greg after his admission reported that his behavior was totally inappropriate. The nurses' notes observed that he could not converse and often screamed and howled with a bizarre loudness. He was thought to be preoccupied with being a superman.

During his first art therapy sessions, Greg sat in a corner on the floor with his back to the group. He copied, in pencil, pictures of sports events, compulsively striving for perfection[1]. However, the rest of the group took little notice of Greg or his drawings.

As the sessions progressed, Greg began to use more floor space and his drawings began to win the group's attention.

His drawings, still in pencil, became bolder, filling more of the page[2]. Group members began responding to his sense of humor.

He stayed well away from the "messy" paint area but began to draw with felt pens. His drawings became less structured and "looser"[3] and he began to respond to the activity of his peers, watching them experiment with paint mixing.

Although he continued to work with felt pens, his drawings became larger and bolder[4]. With more positive response and support, he began to talk about the meaning

CASE 3.   GREG

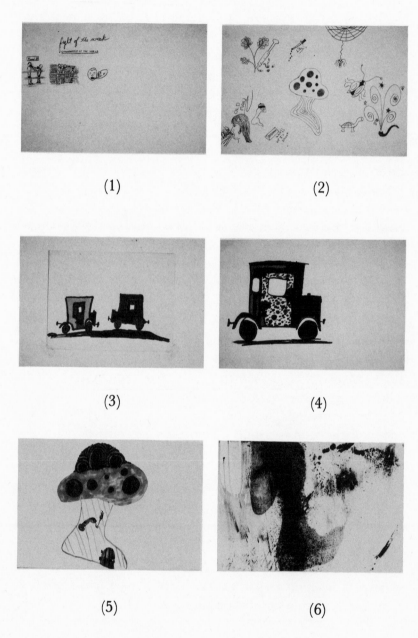

(1)

(2)

(3)

(4)

(5)

(6)

of his drawings, and brought his humor to a verbal level[5]. Slowly, he participated in discussions involving other group members. By his final session, he was able to apply paint to his paper in a free, spontaneous manner, and delighted in the design[6].

RELATING ART WORK TO THE PATIENT'S HISTORY

The interpretation of these paintings and drawings is meaningless unless they are considered in the total clinical past and present makeup of each patient. For example, Greg's final painting was interpreted as welcome progress toward a less inhibited, less withdrawn personality, whereas, the same type of painting by another patient could represent a regression. The fact that Doug might have used a large amount of red paint cannot be interpreted as "aggressive" until the use of the red color is correlated in a meaningful way with what is known about him clinically.

THE ART THERAPIST SHOULD BE A COMPETENT PSYCHOTHERAPIST

The art therapist does not have to be a talented, trained artist, but he should have enough experience with art media to understand the projection of the artist into his art productions and to know what it feels like to reveal innermost thoughts, feelings, and conflicts through graphic expression. Having this kind of personal art experience enables a true empathy with the members of an art therapy group. Personal, individual, and group psychotherapy experience and training, as well as a well-rounded exposure to traditional academic mental health studies all go into making the difference as to whether the art therapist delves into the dynamics of the patients producing graphic revelations about themselves. One cannot just gather a group of patients together, instruct them to paint and draw, and then make far reaching psychodynamic interpretations.

ART THERAPY IS NOT FOR EVERYONE

Not all young patients respond to the invitation of art therapy. Some teenagers become too threatened by the atmosphere of free expression, even though it is really freedom that they say they want so desperately! Self-critical and immature, some adolescent patients are ashamed of their lack of ability to express themselves and suffering with this realization, refuse to attend sessions despite the supportive efforts of the art therapists.

Art therapy is a bridge that patients can cross over to harder-to-reach terrain in treatment. It provides an accepting, pleasurable, nonpressured atmosphere. The adolescents are invited to be uninhibited and "loose" but within a protective boundary of rules that say, "It's safe to be as loose as you can be. We won't let you get so loose that you can hurt each other or yourself—in here!" For many disturbed young people, art therapy is the very beginning of intimate communication with the rest of the world.

Therapeutic Approaches

NORMAN S. BRANDES, M.D. AND
MALCOLM L. GARDNER, PH.D.

Though approaches to the group therapy of adolescent emotional disturbances vary over a wide range, there are several areas of amazing communality in perceptions that therapists hold not only of youth as a group, but also of goals in their treatment. The extended period of dependence to which present day youth are subjected is a phenomena which seems universally viewed as of considerable significance and either because of, or in spite of this, the adolescent is battling with greater intensity than ever before for independence and a piece of the mature action. Therapists, regardless of approach or theoretical framework, have as one of their goals, either explicit or implied, helping the adolescent reach a stage of responsible independence. It is interesting and encouraging that even therapists who work with disturbed adolescents who are social problems still look to youth with confidence and hope to make a better world.

Our introductory chapter points out that "what was typical of youth yesterday is not typical of them today," and talks of the "youth culture" as a modern phenomena. However, the last generation of youth was a "now" generation in its period and those of today are probably destined to have children that, someday, will also be described as "out of this world." To some extent the "generation gap" has been with us in our past and hopefully, provided that comunication across it remains open, will remain with us in the future. Both the old and the young can benefit from reciprocal feedback; it would be a severe blow to progress if the "gap" were closed and a status quo established. Young people have always been more interested in improving the world in which they find themselves than in preserving it as it was presented to them.

ADOLESCENTS IN CROSSFIRE

Adolescents of today's world are in the middle of long established crossfire of demands and expectations. On the one hand, family and society demand that they not act as children, be productive, establish sound moral and sexual attitudes and behavior, and work out their intrapersonal and interpersonal problems of living and identity without too much noise and disturbance. On the other hand, their quest for separation from the family together with their bid for self-recognition and autonomy must go on without forsaking too many of the needs and pleasures they enjoyed from yesterday's childhood. While they enjoy being better educated, better trained, and better moneyed than any previous generation, they condemn the materialism that produces this pleasurable affluent state.

Along with their problems of demand and expectation, today's adolescents are confused about the concept of individualism. This confusion appears, in the interaction between the adolescent and his family and community, with disturbing frequency. He is told, "Be an individual, think for yourself, don't always go along with the group. What if your friends wanted to rob a bank? Does that mean you should rob a bank, too? Make your own decisions. When are you going to grow up and act like an adult?"

The adolescent asks, "Can I become a rugged individualist and fit into my peer group at the same time?" And the answer is, "Be a part of your group, don't be queer and different. If you want to get along in this world, you have to be able to get along in a group. Where the hell is your team spirit?" Long before adolescence, the child whose parents want him to be an individualist and think for himself is started in nursery school one year earlier so he will learn better and faster how to blend in with a group of kids.

GROUP THERAPY OFFERS REALITY TESTING

Out of this conflict and confusion that confronts all "normal adolescents," the disturbed adolescents emerge in greater conflict and confusion. Group therapy is one means of helping them find their individual identities at the same time that they are coping with the many anxieties of finding a place in their peer group. The group therapy experience offers them a chance to see themselves as their peers see them and not just as they distort themselves; it offers the opportunity to come to realistic grips with "Who am I?"—

a question that an isolated, self-effacing, depressed young person has great difficulty understanding, much the less answering. The recent group approaches to treating those who are socially as well as emotionally disturbed also offers them an opportunity to recognize their own problems, become active contributors to their solution, and experience a sense of belonging and value in the social structure.

The chapter on the use of the creative activities of music, dance, and original poetry reading and the chapter on art therapy add dimensions to the group treatment of disturbed adolescents. These nonverbal expressions bring about more looseness, freedom, and spontaneity and, by becoming stimuli and foci for verbal group interaction, help young patients reveal conflicts. Furthermore, engaging in creative activities together enhances group support, understanding, and cohesiveness among the members. These are important events in the lives of those severely disturbed adolescents who suffer a great deal from lack of ordinary communication.

THERAPY MUST BE DIVERSE, EXCHANGEABLE, AND CONNECTING

Like family therapy, artistic activity groups are ideal bridges to other forms of psychotherapy; relatedness is enhanced by these group experiences, helping to prepare the way for traditional individual and group psychotherapy later on (or in many cases, at the same time).

Both the chapters on the use of creativity in groups and the chapter on family treatment indicate that all kinds of emotionally charged material and interactions take place in the sessions. In other words, the groups are not simply intellectual experiences or entertainment, but move into serious and intense levels. They bring into therapy qualities such as despair, loneliness, irrational hostility, and pain that are churning around in the adolescent unconsciousness of their members and which cannot be handled by their everyday life situations.

THE NECESSITY OF AN ADEQUATELY TRAINED THERAPIST

In view of the intensity of emotion which takes place in any group with adolescents, therapists must realize that adequate training and skills in psychodynamics and psychotherapy are not only prerequisite but are of crucial concern. How lack of proper psychological knowledge and skills can precipitate trouble in a group can be found by studying the cases illustrated in the chapter on art therapy. The interpretations of a patient's creative productions are really quite useless, unless the past and present psychological makeup of that patient is known and skillfully worked into the therapy framework. An unskilled or untrained "therapist" can throw oil on burning embers by jumping into the interpretations of these productions without really understanding the patient or what possible effect his interpretations could produce.

WHAT IS THE RESPONSIBILITY OF THE THERAPIST?

The real issue of therapy involves the sense of professional responsibility of the therapist that is not attained simply by assuming and experiencing the role. Helping the young patient to face up to the responsibility for himself, his thoughts, his attitudes, his behavior, and the consequences of these and finally to assume some responsibility to the group is a long-term task for the hard working group therapist. The group therapist is also faced with assuming responsibility for himself. If he has a good, solid training background and takes it with him into the group therapy room, this, alone, does not make him responsible. Obviously, armed with adequate training but without a professional exposure to meaningful supervision in individual and group psychodynamics, the therapist who works with adolescents and young adults in groups will sooner or later have a very difficult, if not totally disastrous time, despite his initial, pleasant anticipation that these are "fun groups." The chapter on the handling of transference and countertransference presents a broad base on which to build a therapist's responsibility.

Polonius' advice to Laertes—this above all, to thine own self be true!—applies to the modern psychotherapist, whether he practices in an individual or group therapy structure. How the therapist gets to know himself is complex and covers many possibilities. Psychotherapy, psychoanalysis, and long-term group psychotherapy experiences are all available within various driving distances of most communities. But the therapist must be able to shed his identification with the image of an all important, all knowing professional long enough to seek out and follow through with this kind of very personal help. In addition, there are opportunities for case supervision by a considerably more experienced therapist. Private case discussions with a colleague, even an occasional private luncheon talk, are most helpful. Professional peer supervision groups are slowly making the mental health scene and the group movement will give greater impetus to them. Lacing a busy appointment schedule with mental health meetings, active participation in seminars to exchange ideas about patient care, and going to periodic training institutes either as trainee or trainer are the very least the therapist can do in the name of responsibility. Hopefully, he will become involved in all of these, or most of them, in order to provide his professional self with the vital crosschecking, self-inquiry, and validation that are so necessary if responsibility is to be realistic.

NOT ALL TRANSFERENCE AND COUNTERTRANSFERENCE IS BAD

Transference and countertransference reactions are not all negative and undesirable, even though awareness and understanding of their meaning remains in the forebrain of the responsible therapist. This same therapist simply cannot hold his pulse, check his respiratory rate, and analyze his reactions every minute of the therapeutic hour to see if he is reacting in a problem-free way to transference or to the impact of his patients. He can no longer afford, in view of the sweeping changes in our society and culture, to simply ask, "What do *you* think?" in response to a patient's reaching out with a question. If he watches himself this closely and is this careful, he will be only partly human by today's standards—like a cold water pipe, rigid and inflexible.

A responsible, conscientious, group therapist for young people can radiate and express warmth, understanding, and closeness and not be afraid to *really care*, even though caring makes him vulnerable to their fate in treatment. Although many older adolescent and young adult patients say they *do*, most of them really *do not* want (and most of them cannot handle) erotic, physical expressions of caring from the therapist. Instead of this, they usually crave a relationship that is trusting, close, warm, sincere, reliable, and accepting, on which they can build emotional strength to change and to grow psychologically. As a result of such qualities in the therapy relationship, not only does the patient grow but throughout a successful therapy so does the therapist.

A beautiful, intelligent, but dejected, lonely young woman felt that all she had "going for her" was her desirability to the opposite sex. Her self-esteem was elevated by the jealousy of other females. Whenever she brought up her caring feelings for her therapist, he gently but firmly reminded her that the purpose of her therapy was not to have a love affair with him but to find out more about herself and her potential as a human being. She wrote the following poem to this therapist:

TEMPTATION

It's not your face that haunts me;
It's the nearness of you.
It's the thoughts of your caress that
sets my soul in mortal conflict.

The battle rages over wanting you and
the desire to touch you
gently, ever gentle:
your lips,
your face, your eyes,
your temple, drowning in delight.

My heightened pulse races out to you
asking your participation
in my life.

This poetic invitation represented a turning point in her therapy since it was used by the therapist to clarify his responsibility to her as well as what her responsibility must be toward her work in therapy. Soon after, she expressed dissatisfaction with her limited educational experience. She enrolled in evening college classes at the end of her work day and began to pursue the study of a writing career.

References

Azima, H., and Azima, Fern J., "Projective Group Therapy," *Int. J. Group Psychother.*, 9:176–183, 1959.

Azima, Fern J., "Interaction and Insight in Group Psychotherapy: The Case for Insight," *Int. J. Group Psychother.*, 19:259–267, 1969.

Boenheim, C., "The Position of Art Therapy Within Contemporary Psychotherapy," *Amer. J. of Art Therapy*, April, 1970.

Brandes, N. S., "Challenges in the Management of Troubled Adolescents," *Clin. Pediat.*, 3:647, 1964.

——— "Understanding the Adolescent in Group Psychotherapy," *Clin. Pediat.*, 4:203, 1965.

———— "Group Psychotherapy for the Adolescent," *Psychiat. Opinion*, 5 : 6, 1968.

———— "The Disturbed Adolescent; Discussion of an Outpatient Psychotherapeutic Approach," *Ohio Med. J.*, 64 : 1272, 1968.

———— "Some Thoughts on Countertransference and Dr. Albert Deutsch," *J. Psychoanal. in Groups*, 2 : 3, 1970.

———— "Group Psychotherapy for the Adolescent" in *Current Psychiatric Therapies*, Vol. II, Jules H. Masserman, ed. New York : Grune & Stratton, Inc., 1971.

Cabot, Diane, "Hotline," *Prince George's County Mental Health Asso.*, Hyattsville, Maryland, 1971.

Couvillon, Bryson, "Proposal for Teenage Pregnancy Prevention Program," *Family Life Asso.* Washington, D.C., 1968.

Durkin, Helen E., "Transference in Group Psychotherapy Revisited," *Int. J. Group Psychother.*, 1 : 11–22, 1971.

Evans, J., "Inpatient Analytic Group Therapy of Neurotic and Delinquent Adolescents: Some Specific Problems Associated with These Groups," *Psychother. Psychosom.*, 13 : 265, 1965.

Freud, A., "Some Recent Developments in Child Analysis," *Psychother. Psychosom.*, 13 : 36, 1965.

Freud, S., *Group Psychology and the Analysis of the Ego.* London : Hogarth Press, 1940.

Geller, J. J., "Group Psychotherapy in Child Guidance Clinics," *Curr. Psychiat. Ther.*, 3 : 219, 1963.

Godenne, G. D., "Outpatient Adolescent Group Psychotherapy, Part I. Review of the Literature on the Use of Co-therapists, Psychodrama, and Parent Group Therapy," *Amer. J. Psychother.*, 18 : 584, 1964.

———— "Outpatient Adolescent Group Psychotherapy, Part II. Use of Co-therapists, Psychodrama, and Parent Group Therapy," *Amer. J. Psychother.*, 19 : 40, 1965.

Handlon, J., and Parloff, M., "The Treatment of Patient and Family as a Group," *Int. J. Group Psychother.*, 12:132–141, April, 1962.

Horwitz, M. J., "Graphic Communication: A Study of Interaction Painting with Schizophrenics," *Amer. J. Psychother.*, Vol. 17, No. 2, April, 1963.

Julian, B., Ventola, L., Christ, J., "Multiple Impact Therapy: The Integration of Young Hospitalized Patients with their Mothers," *Int. J. Group Psychother.*, 19:501–509, Oct., 1969.

Kelly, James, et. al., "Mental Health Programs in the Schools," Conference at the Univ. of Maryland, Nov., 1968.

Kimbro, E., Taschman, H., and Wylie, H., and MacLennan, B., "A Multiple Family Group Approach to Some Problems of Adolescence," *Int. J. Group Psychother.*, 17:18–24, Jan., 1967.

Knorr, N. J., et. al., "Mixed Adult and Adolescent Group Therapy," *Amer. J. Psychother.*, 20:323, 1966.

Koppitz, E. M., *Psychological Evaluation of Children's Human Figure Drawings.* New York: Grune & Stratton, Inc., 1968.

Kraft, I. A., "An Overview of Group Therapy with Adolescents," *Int. J. Group Psychother.*, 18:461, 1968.

Levi, L. D., Stienlin, H., and Savard, R. J., "Fathers and Sons: The Interlocking Crisis of Integrity and Identity," *Psychiatry*, Vol. 34, 1971.

Lewin, K., "Frontiers in Group Dynamics," *Human Relations*, 1:5–41, 1947.

MacLennan, B. W., "Training for New Careers," *Community and Mental Health J.*, 2:135–141, 1966.

——— "The Group as a Reenforcer of Reality," Presented at *Amer. Orthopsychiat. Conference.* Washington, D.C., 1967.

——— "Group Approaches to the Problem of Socially Deprived Youth: The Classical Psychotherapeutic Model," *Int. J. Group Psychother.*, Vol. XVIII, 3:481–494, Oct., 1968.

——— "Mental Health School Collaboration in a Suburban City School System," Magnusson and Quinn, ed. *Mental Health Proposal to the Schools.* Washington, D.C. MSPHS, 1972.

——— and Felsenfeld, N., *Group Counseling and Psychotherapy with Adolescents.* New York: Columbia Univ. Press, 1970.

——— and Klein, W., "The Utilization of Groups in Job Training," *Int. J. Psychother.*, Vol. XV, 4:424–433, Oct., 1965.

Masterson, J. F., Jr., "The Symptomatic Adolescent Five Years Later," *Amer. J. Psychiat.*, 123:11, 1967.

Mitchell, Lonnie, et. al., *Bakers Dozen Neighborhood Program.* Report for the Center for Community Studies, Howard University, 1968.

Moreno, J. L., "The Philosophy of the Moment and the Spontaneity Theatre," *Sociometry*, 4:206–215, 1941.

Namer, Albert and Hartinez, Yolanda, "Case Study: The Use of Painting in Group Psychotherapy with Children," *Bulletin of Art Ther.*, Vol. 6, 2:73–78, 1967.

Naumburg, Margaret, *Dynamically Oriented Art Therapy: Its Principles and Practice.* New York: Grune & Stratton, 1966.

Paul, Norman, "Multiple-Family Therapy: Secrets and Scapegoating in Family Crisis," *Int. J. Group Psychother.*, 20: 37–47, Jan., 1970.

Plokker, J. H., *Art from the Mentally Disturbed.* Boston: Little, Brown & Co., 1965.

Rogers, C. R., *The Process of the Basic Encounter Groups.*

La Jolla, Cal.: Western Behavioral Science Institute, 1968.

Sager, C. J., "A Symposium on Combined Individual and Group Psychotherapy: Insight and Interaction in Combined Therapy," *Int. J. Group Psychother.*, 14:403, 1964.

Scheidlinger, S., "Current Trends in Group Therapy with Children and Adolescents: Introductory Remarks," *Int. J. Group Psychother.*, 18:445, 1968.

Schonfeld, W. A., "Trends in Adolescent Psychiatry," *Curr. Psychiat. Ther.*, 9:52, 1969.

——— "The Adolescent in Contemporary American Psychiatry," *Int. J. Psychiat.*, 5:470, 1968.

Schwartz, E. K., "Group Psychotherapy: The Individual and the Group," *Psychother. Psychosom.*, 13: 142, 1965.

Slavson, S. R., "Para-analytic Group Psychotherapy: A Treatment of Choice for Adolescents," *Psychother. Psychosom.*, 13:321, 1965.

Stein, A., "A Symposium, etc.: The Nature of Transference in Combined Therapy," *Int. J. Group Psychother.*, 14: 413, 1964.

Sullivan, H. S., *Conceptions of Modern Psychiatry.* New York: W. W. Norton, 1953.

Ulman, E., and Levy, I., "An Experimental Approach to the Judgement of Psychopathology from Paintings," *Bulletin of Art Therapy*, Oct., 1968.

INDEX

Preoccupations, 28
Prisons, 35, 36
Probation, 36
Problems
  analysis, 40
  contemporary, 31-44
  social, 69
  youth, 43-44
Professionals, 43
Programs
  mental health, 41-44
  out-of-school, 39
  recreational, 42-44
  school, 41
  youth lead treatment, 34, 40-41
Projection, 107
Psychodramatics, 95-97, 135-136, 138
  see also Acting out
Psychology clubs, 38-39
Psychosis, 68
Psychotherapist, Psychotherapy, see
  Therapist, Therapy
Pupils, see Students

Rapping, 34, 73
Reactions
  hostile, 60
  interpersonal, 94
Readjustment, 85
Reality, 56
  testing, 157-158
Rebellion, 61, 72
Referral, 43
Reform, correctional, 35
Regression, 113, 127-128
Relatedness, human, 99
Relationships, 59, 76
  human, 44
  intrafamilial, 94
  marital, 90, 91, 99
  out-of-group, 56
  primary, 85
Relief, 78
Responses, therapeutic, 33
Responsibility, 65, 80-81
  clarification of, 94
Resistance, 53-57, 61, 64, 69, 80, 107
Retardation, 69
Role playing, 95-97
Role reversal, 95-96
Room, art therapy, 141-142
Running away, 88
Russia, 24, 26

Satisfactions, need, 94-95
Schedules, 48-49, 54, 56, 59
Schism, 98
Schools, 36-38
Seizure, 118-119
Self-esteem, 44
  negative, 98
Self-evaluation, 79
Seminars, 39-40
Sensitivity training, 39
Separation, 85
  and family reconstruction, 91
Sessions
  character of, 64-65
  day-long, 97
  individual, 67, 70, 71-72, 119-121
  time and frequency, 71-72
Sex, 38-39, 88, 132
Significant others, 27
Silence, 64-65, 113-117
Slavson, S. R., 17
Society, rejection by youth, 32-33
Socio-cultural factors, 27-28, 69-70
Socioeconomics, 70
Somatization, 117-119, 121, 125
Stress, 67
Students, 45-61
  ambivalent feelings of, 47-48
  balance of pressures, 49
  bombardment of, 46
  college, 79-80
  depression, 57
  identification, 50
  isolation, 57
  planning, 37
  problems of new, 39-40
  sensitivity, 60
  and society, 47
  togetherness, 47
Subject matter, 55
Suicide, 43, 88
Sulkiness, 117
Support, 56
  emotional, 85-86
Suspiciousness, 64
Symptoms, 78, 98-99, 117
System
  and adolescents, 29-30
  see also Establishment
Systems, family, 83-84

Talking, 114-115, 116
Teaching, 41, 64
Technology, 22, 25, 26